SHIPS
OF OUR ANCESTORS

SHIPS
OF OUR
ANCESTORS

Michael J. Anuta

Originally published 1983 by
Ships of Our Ancestors, Inc.
Menominee, Michigan
Reprinted in 1993, 1996 and 1999 by
Genealogical Publishing Co., Inc.
1001 N. Calvert St., Baltimore, Md. 21202
Library of Congress Catalogue Card Number 93-70622
International Standard Book Number 0-8063-1381-1
Made in the United States of America

Contents

Acknowledgments

Acknowledgment is made of the services, research, and contributions of many museums, studios, historic societies, libraries, and personal collections:

Steamship Historical Society of America, Providence, Rhode Island

University of Baltimore Museum Library, Baltimore, Maryland

Mystic Seaport Museum, Mystic, Connecticut

Mariner's Museum, Newport News, Virginia

National Maritime Museum, Greenwich, England

Oceanic Navigation Research Society, Universal City, California

Peabody Museum of Salem, Salem, Massachusetts

North German Lloyd Line, Herford, Germany

American Historical Society of Germans from Russia, Lincoln, Nebraska

German Russian Heritage Society, Bismarck, North Dakota

All of the Post Card pictures are from the personal collection of Charles Ira Sachs of the Oceanic Navigation Research Society, and their use is gratefully acknowledged.

Special acknowledgment is made of the extensive contributions and research of Mrs. Emma S. Haynes, author, historian, educator, genealogist, translator, and specialist in researching ships and passenger lists. Her enthusiastic support for this project has been most valuable.

Individuals too numerous to mention have also contributed information on ships and voyages. Grateful acknowledgment is made of all assistance and contributions.

Preface

What greater thrill can people experience than to see pictures of the actual ships on which their forebears walked the decks or spent sleepless nights in terror of the ocean, sick at heart about leaving their homes and anxious about the future! Such pictures are a unique reminder of the heroic period of mass migration and the special role of the steamship.

Unfortunately, *Ships of Our Ancestors* is late. It should have been published while the immigrants were still living so the first generation could have learned at first hand more about their cultural heritage and how their forebears met the challenges that brought them across the Atlantic.

Books on ships are numerous; however, no one before has endeavored to assemble pictures of immigrant ships and publish them in a book comprised solely of pictures. The research for the collection covered a period of several years. Photos of some ships are missing or were not available to me when I assembled the collection, but I suspect this album of nearly 900 ships will not disappoint those readers who might be curious about the ships of their ancestors.

Michael J. Anuta

Preface to the Reprint Edition

Ships of Our Ancestors is not a genealogical sourcebook but a compilation of photographs of the steamships that were employed in transporting immigrants to this country in the heyday of mass migration. It was on board the very ships pictured here that immigrants travelled in "steerage," crossing the Atlantic in conditions of extreme discomfort and peril. These were the propeller-driven, steel-hulled leviathans of legend, owned and operated by such famous shipping lines as North German Lloyd, White Star, Cunard, Guion, Red Star, Inman, and Hamburg-American, and in their groaning steerage compartments they transported an ocean of humanity to an uncertain future in America. These were the ships at the very center of the European exodus, the workhorses of mass migration. Without these ships the great Atlantic migration that got underway after the Civil War would never have happened.

How fascinating to see these ships in photographs! How intriguing to think that from the crowded decks of these awesome vessels countless thousands of families embarked on their American odyssey! Equally, it is amazing that photos of so many of these old ships exist, and it is to Michael Anuta that we owe thanks for doggedly tracking them down and ultimately assembling them in this pictorial narrative. A complete photographic archive in itself, photos of nearly 900 ships are arranged here in alphabetical order, and each ship is further identified by date, shipping line, and source. The ships themselves were broken up and sold for salvage long ago, or were wrecked or lost at sea, and the passengers by now have also gone to their rest, but the haunting images of the ships remain.

The genealogist may seek confirmation of an ancestor's migration in documents and passenger lists, but these photographs provide evidence of a different sort; they are a visual testimony of the great passenger ships that grew old in service and then passed from the scene without a trace. They are proof of a bygone time and our connection to it.

Genealogical Publishing Company

SHIPS
OF OUR ANCESTORS

S.S. AACHEN, 1895 North German Lloyd
Courtesy The Peabody Museum of Salem

S.S. ABANGAREZ, 1909 United Fruit Co.
Courtesy The Peabody Museum of Salem

S.S. ABYSSINIA, 1870 Cunard Line
Courtesy Alex Shaw Collection, S.S.H.S. Univ. of Baltimore Library

S.S. ACADIA, Cunard Line
Courtesy of Mystic Seaport Museum, Inc., Mystic, CT

S.S. ACROPOLIS, 1890 Stephen O. Stephenides
Courtesy Steamship Historical Society Collection, Univ. of Baltimore Library

S.S. ADRISTIC, 1871 Red Star Line
Courtesy The Peabody Museum of Salem

S.S. ALASKA, 1882 Guion Line
Courtesy The Peabody Museum of Salem

S.S. ALEPPO, 1865 Cunard Line
Courtesy The Peabody Museum of Salem

S.S. ALESIA, 1906 Fabrc Line
Courtesy The Peabody Museum of Salem

S.S. ALFONSO XII, 1890
Courtesy The Peabody Museum of Salem

S.S. ALFONSO XIII, 1888
Courtesy The Peabody Museum of Salem

S.S. ALGERIA, 1875 Cunard Line
Courtesy The Peabody Museum of Salem

S.S. ALLEMANIA, 1865 Hamburg America Line
Courtesy The Peabody Museum of Salem

S.S. ALLER, North German Lloyd
Courtesy of Mystic Seaport Museum, Inc., Mystic, CT

S.S. AMERICA, 1857 Cunard Line
Courtesy of Mystic Seaport Museum, Inc., Mystic, CT

S.S. AMERICA, 1863 North German Lloyd
Courtesy The Peabody Museum of Salem

S.S. AMERICA, 1884 National S.S. Co.
Courtesy The Peabody Museum of Salem

AMERICA, 1904
Courtesy The Peabody Museum of Salem

S.S. AMERICA, 1905 United States Line
Courtesy The Peabody Museum of Salem

S.S. AMERICA, 1908 Navigazione Generale Italiana
Courtesy Steamship Historical Society Collection, Univ. of Baltimore Library

S.S. AMERICA, 1940 Official USN Photo,
Courtesy Steamship Historical Society Collection, Univ. of Baltimore Library

S.S. AMERIKA, 1872 Thingvilla Line
Courtesy The Peabody Museum of Salem

S.S. AMERIKA, 1905 Hamburg American Line
Courtesy the Peabody Museum of Salem

S.S. AMERIKA, 1905 Hamburg-American Line
Claire White Peterson Photo, Mystic Seaport, Mystic, CT

S.S. AMSTERDAM, 1879 Holland America Line
Courtesy The Peabody Museum of Salem

S.S. ANCHORIA, 1875 Anchor Line
Courtesy The Peabody Museum of Salem

ANDREA DORIA, 1953 Italia Line
Courtesy Steamship Historical Society Collection, Univ. of Baltimore Library

S.S. ANDRE LEBON, 1913 French Line
Courtesy of the Henry W. Uhle Collection, S.S.H.S. Univ. of Baltimore Library

S.S. ANDRE LEBON, 1913 French Line
Courtesy The Peabody Museum of Salem

S.S. ANGLIA, 1864 Anchor Line
Courtesy The Peabody Museum of Salem

S.S. AQUITANIA, 1914 Cunard Line
Courtesy Steamship Historical Society Collection, Univ. of Baltimore Library

S.S. ARABIC, 1903 White Star Line
Courtesy Steamship Historical Society Collection, Univ. of Baltimore Library

S.S. ARAGON, 1905 Royal Mail Line
Courtesy The Peabody Museum of Salem

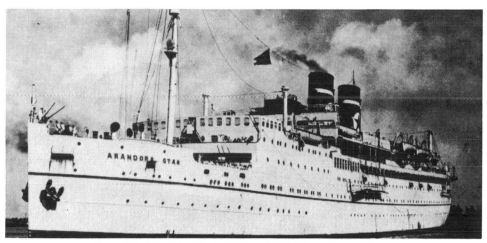

S.S. ARAMDORA STAR, 1927 Blue Star Line
Courtesy Steamship Historical Society Collection, Univ. of Baltimore Library

S.S. ARCADIA, 1896 Hamburg-American Line
Courtesy of Mystic Seaport Museum, Inc., Mystic, Ct

S.S. ARCADIAN, 1899 Royal Mail Line
Courtesy The Peabody Museum of Salem

S.S. ARCTIC, 1849 Collins Line
Courtesy of Mystic Seaport Museum, Inc., Mystic, CT

S.S. ARGENTINA, 1905 La Veloce Line
Courtesy of Mystic Seaport Museum, Inc., Mystic, CT

S.S. ARIZONA, 1879 Guion Line
Courtesy Steamship Historical Society Collection, Univ. of Baltimore Library

S.S. ARMADALE CASTLE, 1903 Union-Castle Line
Courtesy Steamship Historical Society Collection, Univ. of Baltimore Library

S.S. ARMENIA, 1896 Hamburg-American Line
Courtesy Steamship Historical Society Collection, Univ. of Baltimore Library

S.S. ARUNDEL CASTLE, 1921 Union-Castle Line
Courtesy Steamship Historical Society Collection, Univ. of Baltimore Library

S.S. ASAMA MARU, 1929 NYK Line
Courtesy Steamship Historical Society Collection, Univ. of Baltimore Library

S.S. ASCANIA, 1911 Cunard Line
Courtesy The Peabody Museum of Salem

S.S. ASSYRIA, 1908 Anchor Line
Courtesy Steamship Historical Society Collection, Univ. of Baltimore Library

S.S. ASTORIA, 1885 Anchor Line
Courtesy The Peabody Museum of Salem

S.S. ATHLONE CASTLE, 1936 Union-Castle Line
Courtesy Steamship Historical Society Collection, Univ. of Baltimore Library

S.S. ATLANTIC, 1871 White Star Line
Courtesy The Peabody Museum of Salem

S.S. ATLANTIC, 1927 Home Line
Courtesy Steamship Historical Society Collection, Univ. of Baltimore Library

S.S. ATLAS, 1860 Cunard Line
Courtesy The Peabody Museum of Salem

S.S. AUGUSTA VICTORIA, 1888 Hamburg-American Line
Courtesy Steamship Historical Society Collection, Univ. of Baltimore Library

S.S. AUGUSTUS, 1927 Italia Line
Courtesy Steamship Historical Society Collection, Univ. of Baltimore Library

S.S. AUGUSTUS, 1952 Italia Line
Courtesy Steamship Historical Society Collection, Univ. of Baltimore Library

S.S. AURANIA, 1883 Cunard Line
Courtesy The Peabody Museum of Salem

S.S. AURANIA, 1924 Cunard Line
Courtesy The Peabody Museum of Salem

S.S. AUSTRAL, 1881 Orient Line
Courtesy The Peabody Museum of Salem

S.S. AUSTRALIA, 1870 Anchor Line
Courtesy The Peabody Museum of Salem

S.S. AUSTRALIA, 1881 Hamburg American Line
Courtesy The Peabody Museum of Salem

S.S. AVOCA, 1891 New York & Continental Line (British)
Courtesy Alex Shaw Collection, S.S.H.S. Univ. of Baltimore Library

S.S. AVON, 1907 Royal Mail Line
Courtesy Steamship Historical Society Collection, Univ. of Baltimore Library

S.S. AVON, 1907 Royal Mail Line
Courtesy The Peabody Museum of Salem

S.S. BALTIC, White Star Line
Courtesy of Mystic Seaport Museum, Inc., Mystic, CT

S.S. BALTIMORE, North German Lloyd
Courtesy The Peabody Museum of Salem

S.S. BARBAROSSA, 1896 North German Lloyd
Courtesy The Peabody Museum of Salem

S.S. BATAVIA, 1870 Cunard Line
Courtesy The Peabody Museum of Salem

S.S. BATAVIA, 1899 Hamburg-American Line
Courtesy The Peabody Museum of Salem

S.S. BAVARIAN, 1900 Allan Line
Courtesy The Peabody Museum of Salem

S.S. BELGENLAND I, 1878 Red Star-American Line
Courtesy The Peabody Museum of Salem

S.S. BELGENLAND, 1917 Red Star Line
Courtesy The Peabody Museum of Salem

S.S. BELGENLAND, 1917 Red Star Line
Courtesy of Mystic Seaport Museum, Inc., Mystic, CT

S.S. BELGRAVIA, 1899 Anchor Line
Courtesy Steamship Historical Society Collection, Univ. of Baltimore Library

S.S. BERENGARIA, 1912 Cunard Line
Courtesy Steamship Historical Society Collection, Univ. of Baltimore Library

S.S. BERGENSFJORD, 1950 Norwegian American Line
Courtesy Steamship Historical Society Collection, Univ. of Baltimore Library

S.S. BERLIN, 1875 American Line
Courtesy The Peabody Museum of Salem

S.S. BERLIN, 1908, North German Lloyd
Courtesy The Peabody Museum of Salem

S.S. BERMUDIAN, 1904 Quebec Steamship Co.
Courtesy The Peabody Museum of Salem

S.S. BERRIMA, 1913 Peninsular & Oriental Steam Nav. Co.
Courtesy The Peabody Museum of Salem

S.S. BIRMA, 1894 Russian American Line
Courtesy Alex Shaw Collection, S.S.H.S. Univ. of Baltimore Library

S.S. BLUCHER, 1901 Hamburg-American Line
Courtesy The Peabody Museum of Salem

S.S. BOHEMIAN, 1900 Leyland Line
Courtesy The Peabody Museum of Salem

S.S. BONN, 1895 North German Lloyd
Courtesy The Peabody Museum of Salem

S.S. BORUSSIA, 1855 Hamburg-American Line
Courtesy The Peabody Museum of Salem

S.S. BOTHNIA, 1874 Cunard Line
Courtesy The Peabody Museum of Salem

S.S. BRAEMAR CASTLE, 1898 Union Castle Mail S.S. Co.
Courtesy Steamship Historical Society Collection, Univ. of Baltimore Library

S.S. BRANDENBURG, 1901 North German Lloyd
Courtesy Steamship Historical Society Collection, Univ. of Baltimore Library

S.S. BRASIL, 1958 Moore-McCormick Line
Courtesy Steamship Historical Society Collection, Univ. of Baltimore Library

S.S. BRASILIA, 1897 Hamburg-American Line
Courtesy Steamship Historical Society Collection, Univ. of Baltimore Library

S.S. BRASILIAN, 1890 Allan Line
Courtesy The Peabody Museum of Salem

S.S. BRAZIL, 1928 Moore-McCormick Line
Courtesy Steamship Historical Society Collection, Univ. of Baltimore Library

S.S. BREMEN, 1858 North German Lloyd
Courtesy The Peabody Museum of Salem

S.S. BREMEN, 1897 North German Lloyd
Courtesy The Peabody Museum of Salem

S.S. BREMEN, 1929 North German Lloyd
Courtesy Steamship Historical Society Collection, Univ. of Baltimore Library

S.S. BREMEN, 1939 North German Lloyd
Courtesy Steamship Historical Society Collection, Univ. of Baltimore Library

S.S. BRESLAU, 1901 North German Lloyd
Courtesy The Peabody Museum of Salem

S.S. BRITANNIA, 1840 Cunard Line
Courtesy The Peabody Museum of Salem

S.S. BRITANNIC, 1874 White Star Line
Courtesy Steamship Historical Society Collection, Univ. of Baltimore Library

S.S. BRITANNIC, 1914 White Star Line
Courtesy Steamship Historical Society Collection, Univ. of Baltimore Library

S.S. BRITANNIC, 1930 White Star Line
Courtesy Steamship Historical Society Collection, Univ. of Baltimore Library

S.S. BRITISH PRINCE, 1882 American Line
Courtesy The Peabody Museum of Salem

S.S. BRITISH PRINCESS, 1899 British Ship Owners Ltd.
Courtesy Steamship Historical Society Collection, Univ. of Baltimore Library

S.S. BROOKLYN, 1869 Dominion Line
Courtesy The Peabody Museum of Salem

S.S. BUENOS AIRES, 1887 Spanish Line
Courtesy The Peabody Museum of Salem

S.S. BUENOS AYREAN, Allan Line
Courtesy The Peabody Museum of Salem

S.S. BUFFALO, 1885 Wilson Line
Courtesy The Peabody Museum of Salem

S.S. BULGARIA, 1898 Hamburg-American Line
Courtesy Steamship Historical Society Collection, Univ. of Baltimore Library

S.S. BULOW, 1906 North German Lloyd
Courtesy The Peabody Museum of Salem

S.S. BURGUNIDA, 1882, Fabre Line
Courtesy The Peabody Museum of Salem

S.S. CAIRNRONA, 1900 Cairn Line
Courtesy The Peabody Museum of Salem

S.S. CALABRIA, 1857 Cunard Line
Courtesy The Peabody Museum of Salem

S.S. CALABRIA, 1901 Anchor Line
Courtesy The Peabody Museum of Salem

S.S. CALEDONIA, 1904 Anchor Line
Courtesy The Peabody Museum of Salem

S.S. CALEDONIA, 1925 Anchor Line
Courtesy The Peabody Museum of Salem

S.S. CALIFORNIA, 1907 Anchor Line
Courtesy Everett E. Viez Collection, S.S.H.S. Univ. of Baltimore Library

S.S. CALIFORNIA, 1923 Anchor Line
Courtesy r. Loren Graham Collection, S.S.H.S. Univ. of Baltimore Library

S.S. CALIFORNIAN, 1891 Allan Line
Courtesy The Peabody Museum of Salem

S.S. CAMBRIA, 1869 Anchor Line
Courtesy of Mystic Seaport Museum, Inc., Mystic, CT

S.S. CAMBROMAN, 1892 Dominion & Warren Line
Courtesy The Peabody Museum of Salem

S.S. CAMPANIA, 1893 Cunard Line
Courtesy The Peabody Museum of Salem

S.S. CANADA, 1848 Cunard Line
Courtesy The Peabody Museum of Salem

S.S. CANADA, 1865 French Line
Courtesy The Peabody Museum of Salem

S.S. CANADA, 1896 Dominion Line
Courtesy The Peabody Museum of Salem

S.S. CANADA, 1911 Fabre Line
Courtesy of Mystic Seaport Museum, Inc., Mystic, CT

S.S. CANADIAN, 1872 Allan Line
Courtesy The Peabody Museum of Salem

S.S. CANADIAN, 1900 Leyland Line
Courtesy The Peabody Museum of Salem

S.S. CANOPIC, 1900 White Star Line
Courtesy The Peabody Museum of Salem

S.S. CAP ARCONA, 1927 Hamburg-American Line
Courtesy Steamship Historical Society Collection, Univ. of Baltimore Library

S.S. CAP LAY, 1922 French Line
Courtesy The Peabody Museum of Salem

S.S. CAPETOWN CASTLE, 1938 Union Castle Line
Courtesy Steamship Historical Society Collection, Univ. of Baltimore Library

S.S. CARINTHIA, 1895 Cunard Line
Courtesy The Peabody Museum of Salem

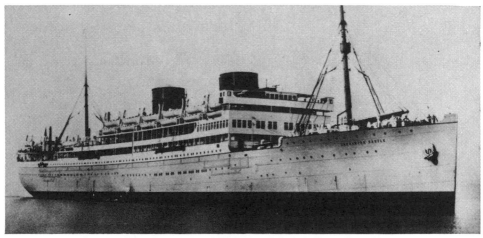

S.S. CARNARVON CASTLE, 1926 Union Castle Line
Courtesy Steamship Historical Society Collection, Univ. of Baltimore Library

S.S. CARONIA, 1905 Cunard Line
Courtesy of the Everett E. Viez Collection, S.S.H.S. Univ. of Baltimore Library

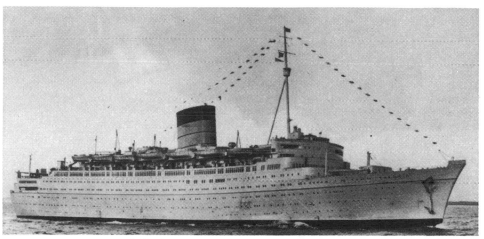

S.S. CARONIA, 1948 Cunard Line
Courtesy Steamship Historical Society Collection, Univ. of Baltimore Library

S.S. CARPATHIA, 1903 Cunard Line
Courtesy The Peabody Museum of Salem

S.S. CARTHAGINIAN, 1884 Allan Line
Courtesy The Peabody Museum of Salem

S.S. CASPIAN, 1870 Allan Line
Courtesy The Peabody Museum of Salem

S.S. CASSEL, 1901 North German Lloyd
Courtesy The Peabody Museum of Salem

S.S. CASTILIAN, 1898 Allan Line
Courtesy Alex Shaw Collection, S.S.H.S. Univ. of Baltimore Library

S.S. CASTILIAN, 1898 Allan Lines
Courtesy The Peabody Museum of Salem

S.S. CATALONIA, 1881, Cunard Line
Courtesy The Peabody Museum of Salem

S.S. CATALUNA, 1883 Spanish Line
Courtesy Alex Shaw Collection, S.S.H.S. Univ. of Baltimore Library

S.S. CEDRIC, 1903 White Star Line
Courtesy of Mystic Seaport Museum, Inc., Mystic, CT

S.S. CELTIC I, 1872 White Star Line
Courtesy The Peabody Museum of Salem

S.S. CELTIC, 1901 White Star Line
Courtesy of Mystic Seaport Museum, Inc., Mystic, CT

S.S. CENTENNIAL STATE, 1921 United States Mail Line
Courtesy Steamship Historical Society Collection, Univ. of Baltimore Library

S.S. CEPHALONIA I, 1882 Cunard Line
Courtesy The Peabody Museum of Salem

S.S. CESTRIAN, 1896 Leyland Line
Courtesy The Peabody Museum of Salem

S.S. Champlain, 1932 French Line
Courtesy Steamship Historical Society Collection, Univ. of Baltimore Library

S.S. CHATEAU LA FITTE, 1881 French Line
Courtesy The Peabody Museum of Salem

S.S. CHESTER, 1873 American Line
Courtesy Alex Shaw Collection, S.S.H.S. Univ. of Baltimore Library

S.S. CHIMBORAZO, 1871 Pacific Steam Navigation Co.
Courtesy The Peabody Museum of Salem

S.S. CHINA, 1862 Cunard Line
Courtesy Steamship Historical Society Collection, Univ. of Baltimore Library

S.S. CHRISTIAN HUYGENS, 1928 Nederland Royal Mail Line
Courtesy Steamship Historical Society Collection, Univ. of Baltimore Library

S.S. CIMBRIA, 1867 Hamburg-American Line
Courtesy The Peabody Museum of Salem

S.S. CIRCASSIA I, 1878 Anchor Line
Courtesy of Mystic Seaport Museum, Inc., Mystic, CT

S.S. CIRCASSIA, 1902 Anchor Line
Courtesy of Mystic Seaport Museum, Inc., Mystic, CT

S.S. CIRCASSIAN, 1873 Allan Line
Courtesy of Mystic Seaport Museum, Inc., Mystic, CT

S.S. CITTA DI MILANO, 1897 La Veloce Line
Courtesy Alex Shaw Collection, S.S.H.S. Univ. of Baltimore Library

S.S. CITTA DI NAPOLI, 1871 La Veloce Line
Courtesy The Peabody Museum of Salem

S.S. CITTA DI TORINO, 1898 La Veloce Line
Courtesy Alex Shaw Collection, S.S.H.S. Univ. of Baltimore Library

S.S. CITY OF ANTWERP, 1867 Inman Line
Courtesy The Peabody Museum of Salem

S.S. CITY OF BALTIMORE, 1854 Inman Line
Courtesy The Peabody Museum of Salem

S.S. CITY OF BERLIN, 1875 Inman Line
Courtesy of Mystic Seaport Museum, Inc., Mystic, CT

S.S. CITY OF BROOKLYN, 1869 Inman Line
Courtesy Steamship Historical Society Collection, Univ. of Baltimore Library

S.S. CITY OF BRUSSELS, 1869 Inman Line
Courtesy The Peabody Museum of Salem

S.S. CITY OF CHESTER, 1873 Inman Line
Courtesy of Mystic Seaport Museum, Inc., Mystic, CT

S.S. CITY OF CHICAGO, 1883 Inman Line
Courtesy The Peabody Museum of Salem

S.S. CITY OF CORK, 1863 Inman Line
Courtesy The Peabody Museum of Salem

S.S. CITY OF LONDON, 1863 Inman Line
Courtesy The Peabody Museum of Salem

S.S. CITY OF MANCHESTER, 1851 Inman Line
Courtesy The Peabody Museum of Salem

S.S. CITY OF MONTREAL, 1872 Inman Line
Courtesy of Mystic Seaport Museum, Inc., Mystic, CT

S.S. CITY OF NEW YORK II, 1865 Inman Line
Courtesy The Peabody Museum of Salem

S.S. CITY OF NEW YORK, 1888 Inman Line
Courtesy Steamship Historical Society Collection, Univ. of Baltimore Library

S.S. CITY OF NEW YORK, 1930 American South Africa Line
Courtesy Steamship Historical Society Collection, Univ. of Baltimore Library

S.S. CITY OF PARIS, 1889 Inman Line
Courtesy The Peabody Museum of Salem

S.S. CITY OF RICHMOND, 1873 Inman Line
Courtesy of Mystic Seaport Museum, Inc., Mystic, CT

S.S. CITY OF ROME, 1881 Inman Line
Courtesy Steamship Historical Society Collection, Univ. of Baltimore Library

S.S. CITY OF WASHINGTON, 1853 Inman Line
Courtesy The Peabody Museum of Salem

S.S. CIUDAD DE CADIZ, 1878 Spanish Line
Courtesy The Peabody Museum of Salem

S.S. CLEVELAND, 1908 Hamburg-American Line
Courtesy of Mystic Seaport Museum, Inc., Mystic, CT

S.S. CLYDE, 1890 Royal Mail Steamship Co.
Courtesy The Peabody Museum of Salem

S.S. COLIMA, 1873 Pacific S.S. Mail Co.
Courtesy Steamship Historical Society Collection, Univ. of Baltimore Library

S.S. COLORADO, 1865 Pacific Mail Steamship Co.
Courtesy The Peabody Museum of Salem

S.S. COLUMBIA I, 1866 Anchor Line
Courtesy The Peabody Museum of Salem

S.S. COLUMBIA, 1889 Hamburg-American Line
Courtesy Steamship Historical Society Collection, Univ. of Baltimore Library

S.S. COLUMBIA, 1902 Anchor Line
Courtesy The Peabody Museum of Salem

S.S. COLUMBUS
Courtesy of Mystic Seaport Museum, Inc., Mystic, CT

S.S. CONSTANTINOPLE, 1896 Greek Line
Courtesy Steamship Historical Society Collection, Univ. of Baltimore Library

S.S. CONSTITUTION, 1951 American Export Line
Courtesy Steamship Historical Society Collection, Univ. of Baltimore Library

S.S. CONTE BIANCAMANO, 1925 Italia Line
Courtesy Steamship Historical Society Collection, Univ. of Baltimore Library

S.S. CONTE GRANDE, 1927 Italia Line
Courtesy Steamship Historical Society Collection, Univ. of Baltimore Library

S.S. CONTE ROSSO, 1922 Lloyd Sabaudo Line
Courtesy Steamship Historical Society Collection, Univ. of Baltimore Library

S.S. CONTE VERDE, 1923 Lloyd Sabaudo Line
Courtesy Steamship Historical Society Collection, Univ. of Baltimore Library

S.S. CORCOVADO, 1907 Hamburg-American Line
Courtesy The Peabody Museum of Salem

S.S. COREAN, 1881 Allan Line
Courtesy The Peabody Museum of Salem

S.S. CORINTHIAN, 1900 Allan Line
Courtesy The Peabody Museum of Salem

S.S. CORSICAN, 1907
Courtesy The Peabody Museum of Salem

S.S. CREFELD, 1895 North German Lloyd
Courtesy The Peabody Museum of Salem

S.S. CRETIC, 1902 White Star Line
Courtesy The Peabody Museum of Salem

S.S. CRISTOFORO COLOMBO, 1953 Italia Line
Courtesy Steamship Historical Society Collection, Univ. of Baltimore Library

S.S. CUBA, 1864 Cunard-New York Line
Courtesy The Peabody Museum of Salem

S.S. CUFIC, 1888 White Star Line
Courtesy The Peabody Museum of Salem

S.S. CUZCO, 1871 Pacific Steam Navigation Co.
Courtesy The Peabody Museum of Salem

S.S. CYMRIC, 1898 White Star Line
Courtesy Steamship Historical Society Collection, Univ. of Baltimore Library

S.S. CZAR, 1912 Russian American Line
Courtesy The Peabody Museum of Salem

S.S. DAMASCUS, 1856 Cunard Line
Courtesy The Peabody Museum of Salem

S.S. DANIA, 1889 Hamburg American Line
Courtesy The Peabody Museum of Salem

S.S. DANTE ALLEGHIERI, 1915 Transatlantca Italina
Courtesy The Peabody Museum of Salem

S.S. DARMSTADT, 1890 North German Lloyd
Courtesy The Peabody Museum of Salem

S.S. DEMERARA, 1872 Cunard Line
Courtesy The Peabody Museum of Salem

S.S. DENMARK, National Line
Courtesy The Peabody Museum of Salem

S.S. DERFFLINGER, 1907 North German Lloyd
Courtesy The Peabody Museum of Salem

S.S. DESEADO, 1912 Royal Mail Line
Courtesy Steamship Historical Society Collection, Univ. of Baltimore Library

S.S. DEUTSCHLAND, 1866 North German Lloyd
Courtesy The Peabody Museum of Salem

S.S. DEUTSCHLAND, 1900 Hamburg-American Line
Courtesy Steamship Historical Society Collection, Univ. of Baltimore Library

S.S. DEUTSCHLAND MAIDEN VOYAGE ARRIVAL NEW YORK HARBOR, JULY 13, 1900

Note Statue of Liberty in Background

Courtesy Albert E. Gayer Collection, Steamship Historical Society University of Baltimore Library

S.S. DEUTSCHLAND APPROACHING PIER 2 HOBOKEN, JULY 13, 1900

Note burned out S.S. SAALE in far background at right

Courtesy Albert E. Gayer Collection, Steamship Historical Society University of Baltimore Library

S.S. DEUTSCHLAND AT PIER 2 HOBOKEN, JULY 13, 1900

Note burned out adjoining North German Lloyd Pier

Courtesy Albert E. Gayer Collection, Steamship Historical Society University of Ealtimore Library

S.S. DEUTSCHLAND DOCKING AT PIER 2 HOBOKEN, JULY 13, 1900
Courtesy Albert E. Gayer Collection, Steamship Historical Society University of Baltimore Library

S.S. DEVONIA, 1877 Anchor Line
Courtesy The Peabody Museum of Salem

S.S. DEVONIAN, 1900 Leyland Line
Courtesy The Peabody Museum of Salem

S.S. DEVONIAN II, 1902 F. Leyland & Co. Ltd.
Courtesy The Peabody Museum of Salem

S.S. DOMINION, 1894 Dominion Line
Courtesy The Peabody Museum of Salem

S.S. DON, 1872 Royal Mail Line
Courtesy The Peabody Museum of Salem

S.S. DONAU, 1868 North German Lloyd
Courtesy The Peabody Museum of Salem

S.S. DOURO, 1865 Royal Mail St. Packet Co.
Courtesy Steamship Historical Society Collection, Univ. of Baltimore Library

S.S. DRESDEN, 1888 North German Lloyd
Courtesy The Peabody Museum of Salem

S.S. DRESDEN, 1914 North German Lloyd
Courtesy Steamship Historical Society Collection, Univ. of Baltimore Library

S.S. DROTTNINGHOLM, 1905 Swedish American Line
Courtesy Steamship Historical Society Collection, Univ. of Baltimore Library

S.S. DUBBELDAM, 1891 Holland American Line
Courtesy The Peabody Museum of Salem

S.S. DUCA D'AOSTA, 1909 Italia Line
Courtesy The Peabody Museum of Salem

S.S. DUCA DEGLI ABRUZZI, 1907 Italia Line
Courtesy The Peabody Museum of Salem

S.S. DUCA DI GENOVA, 1907 Navigazione Generale Italiana
Courtesy The Peabody Museum of Salem

S.S. DUCADI GALLIERA, 1883 La Veloce Line
Courtesy The Peabody Museum of Salem

S.S. DUCHESS DI GENOA, 1883 La Veloce Line
Courtesy The Peabody Museum of Salem

S.S. DUILIO, 1923 Italia Line
Courtesy Steamship Historical Society Collection, Univ. of Baltimore Library

S.S. DUNNOTTAR CASTLE, 1890 Union-Castle Line
Courtesy Steamship Historical Society Collection, Univ. of Baltimore Library

S.S. DUNVEGAN CASTLE, 1896 Union-Castle Line
Courtesy Steamship Historical Society Collection, Univ. of Baltimore Library

S.S. EDINBURGH, 1854 Glasgow-New York Line
Courtesy The Peabody Museum of Salem

S.S. EDINBURGH CASTLE, 1872 Union Castle Mail S.S. Co.
Courtesy The Peabody Museum of Salem

S.S. EDINBURGH CASTLE, 1910 Union Castle Mail S.S. Co.
Courtesy The Peabody Museum of Salem

S.S. EDISON, 1896 Byron S.S. Co.
Courtesy The Peabody Museum of Salem

S.S. EGYPT, 1871 National Line
Courtesy Steamship Historical Society Collection, Univ. of Baltimore Library

S.S. EIDER, 1884 North German Lloyd
Courtesy of Mystic Seaport Museum, Inc., Mystic, CT

S.S. EISENACH, 1908 North German Lloyd
Courtesy The Peabody Museum of Salem

S.S. ELBE, 1881 North German Lloyd
Courtesy of Mystic Seaport Museum, Inc., Mystic, CT

S.S. ELYSIA I, 1872 Anchor Line
Courtesy The Peabody Museum of Salem

S.S. EMPRESS OF AUSTRALIA, 1914 Canadian Pacific Lines
Courtesy The Peabody Museum of Salem

S.S. EMPRESS OF BRITAIN, 1906 Canadian Pacific Lines
Courtesy The Peabody Museum of Salem

S.S. EMPRESS OF BRITAIN, 1955 Canadian Pacific Line
Courtesy of Mystic Seaport Museum, Inc., Mystic, CT

S.S. EMPRESS OF CANADA, 1955 Canadian Pacific Line
Courtesy of Mystic Seaport Museum, Inc., Mystic, CT

S.S. EMPRESS OF FRANCE, 1913 Allan Line
Courtesy The Peabody Museum of Salem

S.S. EMPRESS OF INDIA, 1908 Canadian Pacific Steamships
Courtesy The Peabody Museum of Salem

S.S. EMPRESS OF IRELAND, 1906
Courtesy The Peabody Museum of Salem

S.S. EMPRESS OF JAPAN, 1891 Canadian Pacific Line
Courtesy The Peabody Museum of Salem

S.S. EMPRESS OF SCOTLAND, 1905 Canadian Pacific Lines
Courtesy The Peabody Museum of Salem

S.S. EMS, 1884 North German Lloyd
Courtesy of Mystic Seaport Museum, Inc., Mystic, CT

S.S. ENGLAND, 1863 National Line
Courtesy The Peabody Museum of Salem

S.S. ENTELLA, 1883 Italia Line
Courtesy The Peabody Museum of Salem

S.S. ERIN, 1864 National Line
Courtesy The Peabody Museum of Salem

S.S. ERRA, 1932 Danish East Asiatic Co.
Courtesy of Mystic Seaport Museum, Inc., Mystic, CT

S.S. ESPAGNE, 1909 French Line
Courtesy The Peabody Museum of Salem

S.S. ESPERANZA, 1901 Ward Line
Courtesy The Peabody Museum of Salem

S.S. ETHIOPIA, 1873 Anchor Line
Courtesy The Peabody Museum of Salem

S.S. ETNA, 1855 Cunard Line
Courtesy The Peabody Museum of Salem

S.S. ETRURIA, 1884 Cunard Line
Courtesy Steamship Historical Society Collection, Univ. of Baltimore Library

S.S. EUGENIA, 1906 Unione Austriaco
Courtesy The Peabody Museum of Salem

S.S. EUROPA, 1848 Cunard Line
Courtesy The Peabody Museum of Salem

S.S. EUROPA, 1867 Anchor Line
Courtesy The Peabody Museum of Salem

S.S. EUROPA, 1907 La Veloce Nav. Italiana
Courtesy The Peabody Museum of Salem

S.S. EUROPA, 1930 North German Lloyd
Courtesy of Mystic Seaport Museum, Inc., Mystic, CT

S.S. EXCALIBUR, 1944 American Export Line
Courtesy Steamship Historical Society Collection, Univ. of Baltimore Library

S.S. FERDINAND DE LESSEPS, 1875 French Line
Courtesy The Peabody Museum of Salem

S.S. FINLAND, 1902 Red Star Line
Courtesy The Peabody Museum of Salem

S.S. FLANDRE, 1914 French Line
Courtesy The Peabody Museum of Salem

S.S. FLANDRE, 1952 French Line
Courtesy Steamship Historical Society Collection, Univ. of Baltimore Library

S.S. FLORIDA, 1905 White Star Line
Courtesy The Peabody Museum of Salem

S.S. FLORIDE, 1862 French Line
Courtesy The Peabody Museum of Salem

S.S. FLORIDE, 1907 French Line
Courtesy The Peabody Museum of Salem

S.S. FORT VICTORIA, 1913 Furness, Withy & Co.
Courtesy The Peabody Museum of Salem

S.S. FRANCE, 1865 French Line
Courtesy The Peabody Museum of Salem

S.S. FRANCE, 1912 French Line
Courtesy The Peabody Museum of Salem

S.S. FRANCESCA, 1905 Austro-American Line
Courtesy The Peabody Museum of Salem

S.S. FRANCONIA, 1873 Hamburg-American Line
Courtesy The Peabody Museum of Salem

S.S. FRANCONIA, 1910 Cunard Line
Courtesy The Peabody Museum of Salem

S.S. FRANKFURT, 1899 North German Lloyd
Courtesy The Peabody Museum of Salem

S.S. FREDERICK VIII, 1913 Scandinavian American Line
Courtesy The Peabody Museum of Salem

S.S. FRIEDRICH DER GROSSE, 1896 North German Lloyd
Courtesy The Peabody Museum of Salem

S.S. FRIESLAND, 1889 Red Star Line
Courtesy of Mystic Seaport Museum, Inc., Mystic, CT

S.S. FRISIA, 1872 Hamburg-American Line
Courtesy of Mystic Seaport Museum, Inc., Mystic, CT

S.S. FRISIA, 1909 Konink. Hollendsche Lloyd
Courtesy The Peabody Museum of Salem

S.S. FULDA, 1882 North German Lloyd
Courtesy of Mystic Seaport Museum, Inc., Mystic, CT

S.S. FULDA, 1924 North German Lloyd
Courtesy The Peabody Museum of Salem

S.S. FURNESSIA, 1880 Anchor Line
Courtesy The Peabody Museum of Salem

S.S. FURST BISMARK, 1890 Hamburg-American Line
Courtesy Steamship Historical Society Collection, Univ. of Baltimore Library

S.S. GALLIA, 1878 Cunard Line
Courtesy The Peabody Museum of Salem

S.S. GALLIA, 1883 Cypriene Fabre
Courtesy The Peabody Museum of Salem

S.S. GALLIA, 1914 French Line
Courtesy The Peabody Museum of Salem

S.S. GARIBALDI, 1906 Transatlantic Italiana
Courtesy Alex Shaw Collection, S.S.H.S. Univ. of Baltimore Library

S.S. GELLERT, 1874 Hamburg American Line
Courtesy The Peabody Museum of Salem

S.S. GENERAL VON STEUBEN, 1922 North German Lloyd
Courtesy The Peabody Museum of Salem

S.S. GENERAL WERDER, 1874 North German Lloyd
Courtesy The Peabody Museum of Salem

S.S. GEORGE WASHINGTON, 1908 North German Lloyd
Courtesy The Peabody Museum of Salem

S.S. GEORGIA, 1908 Austro-American Line
Courtesy The Peabody Museum of Salem

S.S. GEORGIC, 1895 White Star Line
Courtesy The Peabody Museum of Salem

S.S. GERA, 1890 North German Lloyd
Courtesy Steamship Historical Society Collection, Univ. of Baltimore Library

S.S. GERMANIA, 1870 Hamburg-American Line
Courtesy The Peabody Museum of Salem

S.S. GERMANIA, 1902 Cypriene Fabre
Courtesy The Peabody Museum of Salem

S.S. GERMANIC, 1874 White Star Line
Courtesy of Mystic Seaport Museum, Inc., Mystic, CT

S.S. GEROLSTEIN, 1904 Bernstein Line
Courtesy The Peabody Museum of Salem

S.S. GERTY, 1903 Austro-American Line
Courtesy The Peabody Museum of Salem

S.S. GIULIO CESARE, 1951 Italia Line
Courtesy Steamship Historical Society Collection, Univ. of Baltimore Library

S.S. GNEISENAU, 1903 North German Lloyd
Courtesy The Peabody Museum of Salem

S.S. GOEBEN, 1906 North German Lloyd
Courtesy The Peabody Museum of Salem

S.S. GOETHE, 1872 Eagle & Hamburg-American Lines
Courtesy The Peabody Museum of Salem

S.S. GOTHIC, 1948 Shaw Savill & Albion Co.
Courtesy Steamship Historical Society Collection, Univ. of Baltimore Library

S.S. GOTHLAND, 1894 Red Star Line
Courtesy The Peabody Museum of Salem

S.S. GOTTARDO, 1883 Italia Line
Courtesy The Peabody Museum of Salem

S.S. GRAF WALDERSEE, 1898 Hamburg-American Line
Courtesy Steamship Historical Society Collection, Univ. of Baltimore Library

S.S. GRAMPIAN, 1907 Allan Line
Courtesy The Peabody Museum of Salem

S.S. GREAT BRITAIN, 1843 Great Western S.S. Co.
Courtesy The Peabody Museum of Salem

S.S. GREECE, 1863 National Line
Courtesy The Peabody Museum of Salem

S.S. GROSSER KURFURST, 1899 North German Lloyd
Courtesy The Peabody Museum of Salem

S.S. GUADELOUPE, 1908 French Line
Courtesy Everett E. Viez Collection, S.S.H.S. Univ. of Baltimore Library

S.S. GUGLIELMO MARCONI, 1963 Lloyd Triestino
Courtesy Steamship Historical Society Collection, Univ. of Baltimore Library

S.S. GUILIA, 1904 Austro-American Line
Courtesy The Peabody Museum of Salem

S.S. GUISEPPE VERDI, 1915, Tranatlantique Italiana
Courtesy Steamship Historical Society Collection, Univ. of Baltimore Library

S.S. HABANA, 1872 Spanish Line
Courtesy The Peabody Museum of Salem

S.S. HAITI, 1913 French Line
Courtesy The Peabody Museum of Salem

S.S. HAMBURG, 1899 Hamburg-American Line
Courtesy The Peabody Museum of Salem

S.S. HAMMONIA, 1854 Hamburg-American Line
Courtesy The Peabody Museum of Salem

S.S. HAMMONIA, 1866 Hamburg-American Line
Courtesy The Peabody Museum of Salem

S.S. HAMMONIA III, 1882 J. & G. Thompson
Courtesy The Peabody Museum of Salem

S.S. HANNOVER, 1899 North German Lloyd
Courtesy The Peabody Museum of Salem

S.S. HANOVERIAN, 1882 Allan Line
Courtesy The Peabody Museum of Salem

S.S. HANOVERIAN, 1902 Leyland Line
Courtesy The Peabody Museum of Salem

S.S. HANSA, 1860 North German Lloyd
Courtesy The Peabody Museum of Salem

S.S. HANSA, 1899 Hamburg-American Line
Courtesy of Mystic Seaport Museum, Inc., Mystic, CT

S.S. HAVEL, 1890 North German Lloyd
Courtesy The Peabody Museum of Salem

S.S. HAVERFORD, 1901 Clydebank American Line
Courtesy The Peabody Museum of Salem

S.S. HECLA, 1860 Anchor Line
Courtesy The Peabody Museum of Salem

S.S. HEKLA, 1884 Thingvalla Line
Courtesy The Peabody Museum of Salem

S.S. HELLIG OLAV, 1902 Scandinavian American Line
Courtesy Steamship Historical Society Collection, Univ. of Baltimore Library

S.S. HELVETIA, 1864 National Line
Courtesy The Peabody Museum of Salem

S.S. HERDER, 1872 Eagle Line
Courtesy The Peabody Museum of Salem

S.S. HERMANN, 1847 Ocean Steam Navigation Co.
Courtesy The Peabody Museum of Salem

S.S. HERMANN, 1865 North German Lloyd
Courtesy The Peabody Museum of Salem

S.S. HESPERIAN, 1908 Allan Royal Mail Line
Courtesy The Peabody Museum of Salem

S.S. HIBERNIAN, 1861 Allan Line
Courtesy The Peabody Museum of Salem

S.S. HIMALAYA, 1949 P & O Line (British)
Courtesy Steamship Historical Society Collection, Univ. of Baltimore Library

S.S. HOHENSTAUFFEN, 1874 North German Lloyd
Courtesy The Peabody Museum of Salem

S.S. HOHENZOLLERN, 1872 North German Lloyd
Courtesy The Peabody Museum of Salem

S.S. HOHENZOLLERN, 1889 North German Lloyd
Courtesy The Peabody Museum of Salem

S.S. HOLLAND, 1858 National Line (British)
Courtesy Alex Shaw Collection, S.S.H.S. Univ. of Baltimore Library

S.S. HOLSATIA, 1868 Hamburg-American Line
Courtesy The Peabody Museum of Salem

S.S. HOMELAND, 1905 Home Lines
Courtesy Steamship Historical Society Collection, Univ. of Baltimore Library

S.S. HOMERIC, 1913 White Star Line
Courtesy The Peabody Museum of Salem

S.S. HUDSON, 1858 North German Lloyd
Courtesy The Peabody Museum of Salem

S.S. HUNGARIAN, 1859 Allan Line
Courtesy The Peabody Museum of Salem

S.S. IBERIA, 1881 Fabre Line
Courtesy Steamship Historical Society Collection, Univ. of Baltimore Library

S.S. IBERIA, 1954 Orient Line (British)
Courtesy Steamship Historical Society Collection, Univ. of Baltimore Library

S.S. ILE DE FRANCE, 1926 French Line
Courtesy Steamship Historical Society Collection, Univ. of Baltimore Library

S.S. ILLINOIS, 1873 American Line
Courtesy Steamship Historical Society Collection, Univ. of Baltimore Library

S.S. ILSENSTEIN, 1904 Bernstein Line
Courtesy The Peabody Museum of Salem

S.S. IMPERATOR, 1912 Hamburg-American Line
Courtesy The Peabody Museum of Salem

S.S. IMPERATRICE EUGENIE, 1866 French Line
Courtesy The Peabody Museum of Salem

S.S. INDEPENDENCE, 1950 American Export Line
Courtesy Steamship Historical Society Collection, Univ. of Baltimore Library

S.S. INDIA, 1869 Anchor Line
Courtesy of Mystic Seaport Museum, Inc., Mystic, CT

S.S. INDIANA, 1873 American Line
Courtesy of Mystic Seaport Museum, Inc., Mystic, CT

S.S. INDIANA, 1905
Courtesy The Peabody Museum of Salem

S.S. INFANTA ISABEL, 1912 Pinillos Izquierdo & Co.
Courtesy The Peabody Museum of Salem

S.S. INFANTA ISABEL DE BORBON, 1913 Spanish Line
Courtesy Everett E. Viez Collection, S.S.H.S. Univ. of Baltimore Library

S.S. IOWA I, 1879 Warren Line
Courtesy The Peabody Museum of Salem

S.S. IOWA, 1902 Warren Line
Courtesy The Peabody Museum of Salem

S.S. IRISHMAN, 1898 Dominion Line
Courtesy The Peabody Museum of Salem

S.S. ISLA DE PANAY, 1882 Transatlantica
Courtesy The Peabody Museum of Salem

S.S. ISLAND, 1882 Thingvalla Line
Courtesy The Peabody Museum of Salem

S.S. ISRAEL, 1955 Zim Israel Navigation Co.
Courtesy Steamship Historical Society Collection, Univ. of Baltimore Library

S.S. ITALIA, 1872 Anchor Line
Courtesy The Peabody Museum of Salem

S.S. ITALIA, 1904 Anchor Line
Courtesy The Peabody Museum of Salem

S.S. ITALIA, 1928 Home Line
Courtesy Everett E. Viez Collection, S.S.H.S. Univ. of Baltimore Library

S.S. ITALY, 1868 National Line
Courtesy The Peabody Museum of Salem

S.S. IVERNIA, 1900 Cunard Line
Courtesy The Peabody Museum of Salem

S.S. JACQUES CARTIER, 1908 French Line
Courtesy The Peabody Museum of Salem

S.S. JAN PIETERSZOON COEN, 1915 Nederland Royal Mail Line
Courtesy The Peabody Museum of Salem

S.S. JAVA, 1865 Cunard Line
Courtesy The Peabody Museum of Salem

S.S. JERUSALEM, 1913 Zim Isreal Nav. Co.
Courtesy The Peabody Museum of Salem

S.S. JERUSALEM, 1957 Zim Israel Navigation Co.
Courtesy Steamship Historical Society Collection, Univ. of Baltimore Library

S.S. JOHN BELL, 1854 Anchor Line
Courtesy The Peabody Museum of Salem

S.S. JUSTICIA, 1915 White Star Line
Courtesy The Peabody Museum of Salem

S.S. KAISER FRIEDRICH, 1898 Hamburg-American Line
Courtesy The Peabody Museum of Salem

S.S. KAISER WILHEM II, 1889, North German Lloyd
Courtesy The Peabody Museum of Salem

S.S. KAISER WILHELM II, 1903 North German Lloyd
Courtesy Steamship Historical Society Collection, Univ. of Baltimore Library

S.S. KAISER WILHELM DER GROSSE, 1897 North German Lloyd
Courtesy Steamship Historical Society Collection, Univ. of Baltimore Library

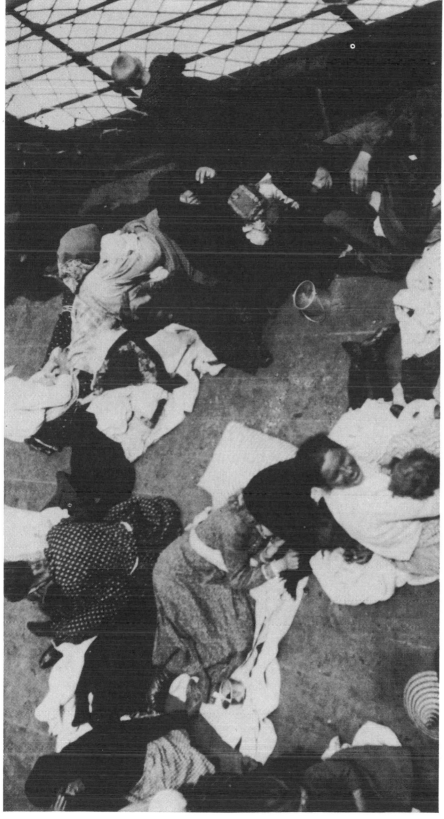

STEERAGE PASSENGERS AT SEA CA. 1902
S.S. KAISER WILHELM DER GROSSE
Courtesy Albert E. Gayer Collection, Steamship Historical Society University of Baltimore Library

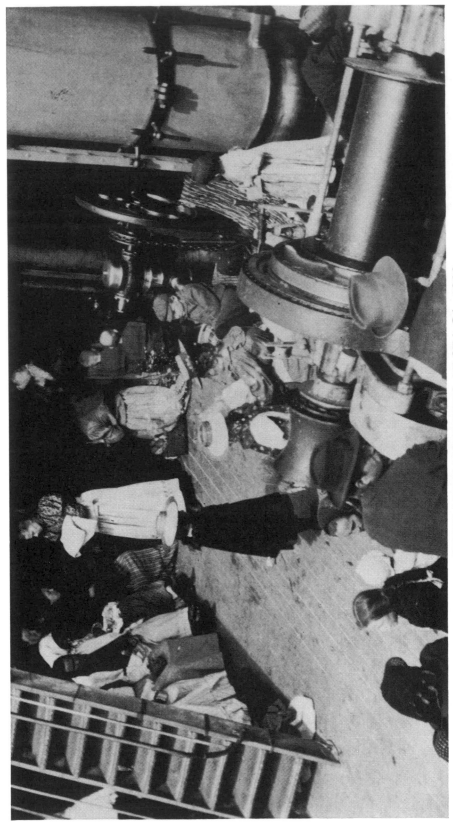

**STEERAGE PASSENGERS AT SEA CA. 1902
S.S. KAISER WILHELM DER GROSSE**
Courtesy Albert E. Gayer Collection, Steamship Historical Society University of Baltimore Library

STEERAGE PASSENGERS AT SEA CA. 1902
S.S. KAISER WILHELM DER GROSSE
Courtesy Albert E. Gayer Collection, Steamship Historical Society University of Baltimore Library

STEERAGE PASSENGERS AT SEA CA. 1902
S.S. KAISER WILHELM DER GROSSE
Courtesy Albert E. Gayer Collection, Steamship Historical Society University of Baltimore Library

STEERAGE PASSENGERS AT SEA CA. 1902, S.S. KAISER WILHELM DER GROSSE VIEW OF STEERAGE FROM 1st CLASS DECK

Courtesy Albert E. Gayer Collection, Steamship Historical Society University of Baltimore Library

S.S. KAISERIN AUGUSTE VICTORIA, 1905 Hamburg-American Line
Courtesy The Peabody Museum of Salem

S.S. KAISERIN MARIA THERESIA, 1890 North German Lloyd
Courtesy The Peabody Museum of Salem

S.S. KANGAROO, 1853 Inman Line
Courtesy The Peabody Museum of Salem

S.S. KANSAS, 1882 Warren Line
Courtesy The Peabody Museum of Salem

S.S. KARLSRUHE, 1889 North German Lloyd
Courtesy The Peabody Museum of Salem

S.S. KARLSRUHE, 1900 North German Lloyd
Courtesy The Peabody Museum of Salem

S.S. KEDAR, 1860 Cunard Line
Courtesy The Peabody Museum of Salem

S.S. KENSINGTON, 1894 American Line
Courtesy The Peabody Museum of Salem

S.S. KIAUTSCHOU, 1900 Hamburg-American Line
Courtesy The Peabody Museum of Salem

S.S. KING ALEXANDER, 1908 Greek Line
Courtesy The Peabody Museum of Salem

S.S. KLEIST 1906 North German Lloyd
Courtesy The Peabody Museum of Salem

S.S. KLOPSTOCK, 1872 Hamburg-American Line
Courtesy The Peabody Museum of Salem

S.S. KOLN, 1899 North German Lloyd
Courtesy The Peabody Museum of Salem

S.S. KONIG ALBERT, 1899 North German Lloyd
Courtesy The Peabody Museum of Salem

S.S. KONIG FRIEDRICH AUGUST, 1906 Hamburg-American Line
Courtesy The Peabody Museum of Salem

S.S. KONIG WILLHELM II, 1907 Hamburg-American Line
Courtesy The Peabody Museum of Salem

S.S. KONIGEN LUISE, 1896 Norddeutscher Lloyd
Courtesy The Peabody Museum of Salem

S.S. KONIGSTEIN, 1907 Bernstein Line
Courtesy Alex Shaw Collection, S.S.H.S. Univ. of Baltimore Library

S.S. KONINGEN EMMA, 1913 Nederland Royal Mail Line
Courtesy The Peabody Museum of Salem

S.S. KOSCUISZKO, 1915 Gdynia American Line
Courtesy The Peabody Museum of Salem

S.S. KRISTIANAFJORD, 1913 Norwegian American Line
Courtesy The Peabody Museum of Salem

S.S. KRONPRINZ WILHELM, 1901 North German Lloyd
Courtesy of Mystic Seaport Museum, Inc., Mystic, CT

S.S. KRONPINZESSIN CECILIE, 1906 North German Lloyd
Courtesy The Peabody Museum of Salem

S.S. KROONLAND, 1902 Red Star Line
Courtesy The Peabody Museum of Salem

S.S. KUNGSHOLM, 1902 Swedish American Line
Courtesy The Peabody Museum of Salem

S.S. KUNGSHOLM, 1928 Swedish American Line
Courtesy Steamship Historical Society Collection, Univ. of Baltimore Library

S.S. KURSK, 1910 Russian American Line
Courtesy The Peabody Museum of Salem

S.S. LA BOURDONNAIS, 1904 French Line
Courtesy The Peabody Museum of Salem

S.S. LA BOURGOYNE, 1886 French Line
Courtesy The Peabody Museum of Salem

S.S. LABRADOR, 1865 French Line
Courtesy The Peabody Museum of Salem

S.S. LABRADOR, 1891 Dominion Line
Courtesy The Peabody Museum of Salem

S.S. LA BRETAGNE, 1886 French Line
Courtesy The Peabody Museum of Salem

S.S. LA CHAMPAGNE, 1886 French Line
Courtesy The Peabody Museum of Salem

S.S. LACONIA, 1912 Cunard Line
Courtesy The Peabody Museum of Salem

S.S. LACONIA, 1922 Cunard Line
Courtesy The Peabody Museum of Salem

S.S. LADY HAWKINS, 1928 Canadian National Line
Courtesy Steamship Historical Society Collection, Univ. of Baltimore Library

S.S. LAFAYETTE, 1864 French Line
Courtesy The Peabody Museum of Salem

S.S. LA GASCOGNE, 1886 French Line
Courtesy The Peabody Museum of Salem

S.S. LA GUARDIA, 1944 American Export Lines
Courtesy The Peabody Museum of Salem

S.S. LAHN, 1837 North German Lloyd
Courtesy Steamship Historical Society Collection, Univ. of Baltimore Library

S.S. LAKE CHAMPLAIN, 1874 Beaver Line
Courtesy The Peabody Museum of Salem

S.S. LAKE CHAMPLAIN, 1900 Canadian Pacific S.S. Co.
Courtesy The Peabody Museum of Salem

S.S. LAKE ERIE, 1900 Allan Line
Courtesy The Peabody Museum of Salem

S.S. LAKE HURON, 1881 Beaver Line
Courtesy The Peabody Museum of Salem

S.S. LAKE MANITOBA, 1880 Beaver Line
Courtesy The Peabody Museum of Salem

S.S. LAKE MANITOBA, 1901 Canadian Pacific Railway Co.
Courtesy The Peabody Museum of Salem

S.S. LAKE MEGANTIC, 1884 Beaver Line
Courtesy Alex Shaw Collection, S.S.H.S. Univ. of Baltimore Library

S.S. LAKE NEPIGON, 1875 Beaver Line
Courtesy The Peabody Museum of Salem

S.S. LAKE ONTARIO, 1887 Beaver Line
Courtesy The Peabody Museum of Salem

S.S. LAKE SIMCOE, 1884 Beaver Line
Courtesy The Peabody Museum of Salem

S.S. LAKE SUPERIOR, 1885 Beaver Line
Courtesy The Peabody Museum of Salem

S.S. LA NAVARRE, 1893 Compagnie Generale Transatlantique
Courtesy The Peabody Museum of Salem

S.S. LANCASTRIA, 1922 Cunard Line
Courtesy Steamship Historical Society Collection, Univ. of Baltimore Library

S.S. LA NORMANDIE, 1882 French Line
Courtesy The Peabody Museum of Salem

S.S. LAPLAND, 1908 Red Star Line
Courtesy The Peabody Museum of Salem

S.S. LA PROVENCE, 1905 French Line
Courtesy The Peabody Museum of Salem

S.S. L'AQUITANE, 1890 French Line
Courtesy The Peabody Museum of Salem

S.S. LA SAVOIE, 1901 French Line
Courtesy The Peabody Museum of Salem

S.S. LA TOURAINE, 1890 French Line
Courtesy The Peabody Museum of Salem

S.S. LAURA, 1907 Austro American Line
Courtesy The Peabody Museum of Salem

S.S. LAURENTIAN, 1872 Allan Line
Courtesy The Peabody Museum of Salem

S.S. LAURENTIC, 1908 White Star Line
Courtesy The Peabody Museum of Salem

S.S. LAYFAYETTE, 1915 Tranatlantique
Courtesy The Peabody Museum of Salem

S.S. LAZIO, 1899 Navigazione Generale Italiana
Courtesy The Peabody Museum of Salem

S.S. LECONTE DELISLE, 1922 French Line
Courtesy Steamship Historical Society Collection, Univ. of Baltimore Library

S.S. LEERDAM, 1882 Holland American Line
Courtesy The Peabody Museum of Salem

S.S. LEERDAM, 1921 Holland American Line
Courtesy The Peabody Museum of Salem

S.S. LEGAZPI, 1904 Spanish Royal Line
Courtesy The Peabody Museum of Salem

S.S. LEIPZIG, 1869 North German Lloyd
Courtesy The Peabody Museum of Salem

S.S. LEON XIII, 1888 Spanish Mail Line
Courtesy The Peabody Museum of Salem

S.S. LEONARDO DA VINCI, 1925 Transatlantica Italiana
Courtesy The Peabody Museum of Salem

S.S. LEONARDO DA VINCI, 1960
Courtesy Steamship Historical Society Collection, Univ. of Baltimore Library

S.S. LESSING, 1874 Hamburg-American Line
Courtesy The Peabody Museum of Salem

S.S. LETITIA, 1912 Anchor Donaldson Line
Courtesy The Peabody Museum of Salem

S.S. L'EUROPE, 1865 French Line
Courtesy The Peabody Museum of Salem

S.S. LEVIATHAN, 1914 U.S. Lines
Courtesy The Peabody Museum of Salem

S.S. LIBERTE, 1928 French Line
Courtesy The Peabody Museum of Salem

S.S. LIGURIA, 1901 Navigazione Generale Italiana
Courtesy The Peabody Museum of Salem

S.S. LIVONIAN, 1881 Allan Line
Courtesy The Peabody Museum of Salem

S.S. LOMBARDIA, 1901 Navigazione Generale Italiana
Courtesy The Peabody Museum of Salem

S.S. LONE STAR STATE, 1921 United States Line
Courtesy Alex Shaw Collection, S.S.H.S. Univ. of Baltimore Library

S.S. LORRAINE, 1900 French Line
Courtesy The Peabody Museum of Salem

S.S. LOUISIANE, 1862 French Line
Courtesy The Peabody Museum of Salem

S.S. LUCANIA, 1893 Cunard Line
Courtesy The Peabody Museum of Salem

S.S. LUDGATE HILL, 1881 Allan Line
Courtesy The Peabody Museum of Salem

S.S. LUETZOW, 1908 North German Lloyd
Courtesy of Mystic Seaport Museum, Inc., Mystic, CT

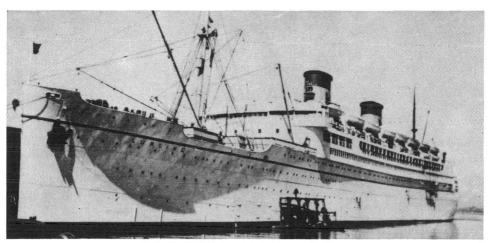

S.S. LURLINE, 1932 Greek Line
Courtesy Steamship Historical Society Collection, Univ. of Baltimore Library

S.S. LUSITANIA, 1871 Beaver Line
Courtesy The Peabody Museum of Salem

S.S. LUSITANIA, 1907 Cunard Line
Courtesy The Peabody Museum of Salem

S.S. LYDIAN MONARCH, 1881 Wilson Line (British)
Courtesy Alex Shaw Collection, S.S.H.S. Univ. of Baltimore Library

S.S. MAAS, 1872 Holland America Line
Courtesy The Peabody Museum of Salem

S.S. MAASDAM, 1871 White Star Line
Courtesy The Peabody Museum of Salem

S.S. MAASDAM, 1952 Holland America Line
Courtesy Everett E. Viez Collection, S.S.H.S. Univ. of Baltimore Library

S.S. MACEDONIA, 1912 National Greek Line
Courtesy, T.H. Franklin Collection, S.S.H.S. Univ. of Baltimore Library

S.S. MACORIS, 1902 French Line
Courtesy The Peabody Museum of Salem

S.S. MADONNA, 1905 Fabre Line
Courtesy The Peabody Museum of Salem

S.S. MAIN, 1868 North German Lloyd
Courtesy The Peabody Museum of Salem

S.S. MAIN, 1899 North German Lloyd
Courtesy The Peabody Museum of Salem

S.S. MAJESTIC, 1890 White Star Line
Courtesy The Peabody Museum of Salem

S.S. MAJESTIC, 1921 White Star Line
Courtesy Steamship Historical Society Collection, Univ. of Baltimore Library

S.S. MALWA, 1908 P & O Line
Courtesy The Peabody Museum of Salem

S.S. MANCHURIA, 1904 American Line
Courtesy The Peabody Museum of Salem

S.S. MANHATTAN, 1866 Guion Line
Courtesy The Peabody Museum of Salem

S.S. MANHATTAN, 1932 United States Line
Courtesy Steamship Historical Society Collection, Univ. of Baltimore Library

S.S. MANILLA, 1873 Italia Line
Courtesy The Peabody Museum of Salem

S.S. MANITOBA, 1892 Atlantic Transport Co., Ltd.
Courtesy The Peabody Museum of Salem

S.S. MANITOU, 1898 Atlantic Transport Line
Courtesy The Peabody Museum of Salem

S.S. MANUEL CALVO, 1892 Compania Transatlantique
Courtesy The Peabody Museum of Salem

S.S. MARATHON, 1860 Cunard Line
Courtesy The Peabody Museum of Salem

S.S. MARCO MINGHETTI, 1876 Italia Line
Courtesy The Peabody Museum of Salem

S.S. MARCO POLO, 1942 Italia Line
Courtesy The Peabody Museum of Salem

S.S. MARGLEN, 1898 Canadian Pacific Steamships
Courtesy The Peabody Museum of Salem

S.S. MARIPOSA, 1883 Oceanic Steamship Co.
Courtesy The Peabody Museum of Salem

S.S. MARIPOSA, 1931 Oceanic Steamship Co.
Courtesy The Peabody Museum of Salem

S.S. MARLOCH, 1904 Canadian Pacific Steamships
Courtesy The Peabody Museum of Salem

S.S. MARNIX VAN SINT ALDEGONDE, 1930 Netherlands Royal Mail Line
Courtesy Steamship Historical Society Collection, Univ. of Baltimore Library

S.S. MARQUES DE COMILLAS, 1928 Spanish Line
Courtesy Alex Shaw Collection, S.S.H.S. Univ. of Baltimore Library

S.S. MARQUETTE, 1898 Atlantic Transport Line
Courtesy The Peabody Museum of Salem

S.S. MARTELLO, 1884 Wilson Line (British)
Courtesy Henry W. Uhle Collection, S.S.H.S. Univ. of Baltimore Library

S.S. MARTHA WASHINGTON, 1908 Austro-American Line
Courtesy The Peabody Museum of Salem

S.S. MARTINIQUE, 1883 French Line
Courtesy The Peabody Museum of Salem

S.S. MARVALE, 1907 Canadian Pacific Line
Courtesy The Peabody Museum of Salem

S.S. MASSACHUSETTS, 1892 Atlantic Transport Co., Ltd.
Courtesy The Peabody Museum of Salem

S.S. MASSILIA, 1902 Anchor Line
Courtesy The Peabody Museum of Salem

S.S. MAURETANIA, 1907 Cunard Line
Courtesy Steamship Historical Society Collection, Univ. of Baltimore Library

S.S. MAURETANIA, 1939 Cunard Line
Courtesy Steamship Historical Society Collection, Univ. of Baltimore Library

S.S. MAYFLOWER, 1902 Dominion Line
Courtesy The Peabody Museum of Salem

S.S. MEDIA, 1947 Cunard Line
Courtesy Steamship Historical Society Collection, Univ. of Baltimore Library

S.S. MEDWAY, 1877 Royal Mail Line
Courtesy The Peabody Museum of Salem

S.S. MEGANTIC, 1909 White Star Line
Courtesy The Peabody Museum of Salem

S.S. MEKNES, 1913 French Line
Courtesy The Peabody Museum of Salem

S.S. MELITA, 1918 Canadian Pacific Steamships
Courtesy The Peabody Museum of Salem

S.S. MENDONZA, 1904 Lloyd Italiano
Courtesy The Peabody Museum of Salem

S.S. MENOMINEE, 1897 Atlantic Transport Co., Ltd.
Courtesy The Peabody Museum of Salem

S.S. MENOMINEE, Red Star Line
Courtesy The Peabody Museum of Salem

S.S. MERION, American Line
Courtesy The Peabody Museum of Salem

S.S. MESABA, 1898 Atlantic Transport Line
Courtesy The Peabody Museum of Salem

S.S. METAGAMA, 1915 Canadian Pacific Steamships
Courtesy The Peabody Museum of Salem

S.S. MEXICO, 1884 Compania Mexicana Transatlantica
Courtesy The Peabody Museum of Salem

S.S. MEXIQUE, 1915 French Line
Courtesy The Peabody Museum of Salem

S.S. MICHIGAN, 1887 Warren Line
Courtesy The Peabody Museum of Salem

S.S. MICHIGAN, 1890 Atlantic Transport Line
Courtesy Steamship Historical Society Collection, Univ. of Baltimore Library

S.S. MILWAUKEE, 1897 Canadian Pacific Railway Co.
Courtesy The Peabody Museum of Salem

S.S. MILWAUKEE, 1929 Hamburg-American Line
Courtesy Steamship Historical Society Collection, Univ. of Baltimore Library

S.S. MINNEAPOLIS, 1900 Atlantic Transport Co. Ltd.
Courtesy The Peabody Museum of Salem

S.S. MINNEDOSA, 1918 Canadian Pacific S.S.
Courtesy The Peabody Museum of Salem

S.S. MINNEHAHA, 1900 Atlantic Transport Line
Courtesy The Peabody Museum of Salem

S.S. MENNEKAHDA, 1917 Atlantic Transport Line
Courtesy The Peabody Museum of Salem

S.S. MINNESOTA, 1866 Warren Line
Courtesy The Peabody Museum of Salem

S.S. MINNESOTA, 1901 Atlantic Transport Co. Ltd.
Courtesy The Peabody Museum of Salem

S.S. MINNETONKA, 1902 Atlantic Transport Line
Courtesy Steamship Historical Society Collection, Univ. of Baltimore Library

S.S. MINNETONKA I, 1902 Atlantic Transport Co. Ltd.
Courtesy The Peabody Museum of Salem

S.S. MINNEWASKA, 1894 Atlantic Transport Line
Courtesy Steamship Historical Society Collection, Univ. of Baltimore Library

S.S. MINNEWASKA, 1909 French Line
Courtesy The Peabody Museum of Salem

S.S. MISSANABLE, 1914 Canadian Pacific Steamship Ltd.
Courtesy The Peabody Museum of Salem

S.S. MISSISSIPPI, 1871 Dominion Line
Courtesy The Peabody Museum of Salem

S.S. MISSISSIPPI, 1903 Atlantic Transport Line
Courtesy The Peabody Museum of Salem

S.S. MOBILE, 1893 Atlantic Transport Co.
Courtesy The Peabody Museum of Salem

S.S. MOHAWK, 1892 Atlantic Transport Co. Ltd.
Courtesy The Peabody Museum of Salem

S.S. MOLTKE, 1901 Hamburg-American Line
Courtesy of Mystic Seaport Museum, Inc., Mystic, CT

S.S. MONGOLIA, 1905 Pacific M.S.S. Co.
Courtesy The Peabody Museum of Salem

S.S. MONGOLIAN, 1891 Allan Line
Courtesy The Peabody Museum of Salem

S.S. MONTACALM, 1921 Canadian Pacific Line
Courtesy The Peabody Museum of Salem

S.S. MONTANA, 1872 Guion Line
Courtesy The Peabody Museum of Salem

S.S. MONTCALM, 1897 Canadian Pacific Railway
Courtesy The Peabody Museum of Salem

S.S. MONTEAGLE, 1899 Canadian Pacific Railway Co.
Courtesy The Peabody Museum of Salem

S.S. MONTEREY, 1897 Canadian Pacific Line
Courtesy Alex Shaw Collection, S.S.H.S. Univ. of Baltimore Library

S.S. MONTE ROSA, 1930 Hamburg-American Line
Courtesy Steamship Historical Society Collection, Univ. of Baltimore Library

S.S. MONTE VIDEAN, 1887 Allan Line
Courtesy The Peabody Museum of Salem

S.S. MONTEVIDEO, 1889 Spanish Line
Courtesy The Peabody Museum of Salem

S.S. MONTEZUMA, 1899 Canadian Pacific Railway Co.
Courtesy The Peabody Museum of Salem

S.S. MONTFORT, 1899 Canadian Pacific Railway Co.
Courtesy The Peabody Museum of Salem

S.S. MONTNAIRN, 1908 Canadian Pacific Steamships
Courtesy The Peabody Museum of Salem

S.S. MONTREAL, 1896 French Line
Courtesy The Peabody Museum of Salem

S.S. MONTREAL, 1900 Canadian Pacific Steamships
Courtesy The Peabody Museum of Salem

S.S. MONTREAL, 1906 Canadian Pacific Line
Courtesy The Peabody Museum of Salem

S.S. MONTROSE, 1897 Canadian Pacific Line
Courtesy Steamship Historical Society Collection, Univ. of Baltimore Library

S.S. MONTROSE, 1922 Canadian Pacific Line
Courtesy Henry W. Uhle Collection, S.S.H.S. Univ. of Baltimore Library

S.S. MONTROYAL, 1906 Canadian Pacific Steamship Ltd.
Courtesy The Peabody Museum of Salem

S.S. MONTSERRAT, 1889 Spanish Line
Courtesy The Peabody Museum of Salem

S.S. MOOLTAN, 1923 P & O Line
Courtesy The Peabody Museum of Salem

S.S. MORAVIA, 1883 Hamburg-American Line
Courtesy Steamship Historical Society Collection, Univ. of Baltimore Library

S.S. MOREAS, 1902 Byron S.S. Co.
Courtesy The Peabody Museum of Salem

S.S. MORIVIAN, 1864 Allan Line
Courtesy The Peabody Museum of Salem

S.S. MORRO CASTLE, 1930 Ward Line
Courtesy Steamship Historical Society Collection, Univ. of Baltimore Library

S.S. MOSEL, 1872 North German Lloyd
Courtesy The Peabody Museum of Salem

S.S. MOUNT CLAY, 1904 United American Line
Courtesy The Peabody Museum of Salem

S.S. MOUNT CLINTON, 1921 United American Lines
Courtesy Steamship Historical Society Collection, Univ. of Baltimore Library

S.S. MOUNT TEMPLE, 1901 Canadian Pacific R.R. Co.
Courtesy The Peabody Museum of Salem

S.S. MUNCHEN, 1922 North German Lloyd
Courtesy Steamship Historical Society Collection, Univ. of Baltimore Library

S.S. NECKAR, 1874 North German Lloyd
Courtesy The Peabody Museum of Salem

S.S. NECKAR, 1910 North German Lloyd
Courtesy The Peabody Museum of Salem

S.S. NEDERLAND, 1873 Red Star Line
Courtesy The Peabody Museum of Salem

S.S. NEPTUNIA, 1920 Greek Line
Courtesy Steamship Historical Society Collection, Univ. of Baltimore Library

S.S. NESTORIAN, 1866 Allan Line
Courtesy The Peabody Museum of Salem

S.S. NEUSTRIA, 1883 Cyprien Fabre & Co.
Courtesy The Peabody Museum of Salem

S.S. NEVADA, 1869 Guion Line
Courtesy The Peabody Museum of Salem

S.S. NEW ENGLAND, 1898 Dominion Line
Courtesy The Peabody Museum of Salem

S.S. NEW YORK, 1858 North German Lloyd
Courtesy The Peabody Museum of Salem

S.S. NEW YORK, 1864 Pacific Mail Steamship Co.
Courtesy The Peabody Museum of Salem

S.S. NEW YORK, 1888 American Line
Courtesy The Peabody Museum of Salem

S.S. NEW YORK, 1922 Greek Line
Courtesy Steamship Historical Society Collection, Univ. of Baltimore Library

S.S. NEW YORK, 1927 Hamburg-American Line
Courtesy Mariners Museum, Newport News, Virginia

S.S. NIAGARA, 1848 Cunard Line
Courtesy The Peabody Museum of Salem

S.S. NIAGARA, 1908 French Line
Courtesy The Peabody Museum of Salem

S.S. NIEUW AMSTERDAM, 1906 Holland American Line
Courtesy The Peabody Museum of Salem

S.S. NOORDAM, 1902 Holland America Line
Courtesy The Peabody Museum of Salem

S.S. NOORDLAND, 1884 Red Star Line
Courtesy The Peabody Museum of Salem

S.S. NORD AMERICA, 1882 La Veloce Line
Courtesy Steamship Historical Society Collection, Univ. of Baltimore Library

S.S. NORMANDIE, 1935 French Line
Courtesy Steamship Historical Society Collection, Univ. of Baltimore Library

S.S. NORMANNIA, 1890 Hamburg-American Line
Courtesy of Mystic Seaport Museum, Inc., Mystic, CT

S.S. NORSEMAN, 1882 Dominion Line
Courtesy The Peabody Museum of Salem

S.S. NORSEMAN, 1897 British Navy Line
Courtesy The Peabody Museum of Salem

S.S. NORTH AMERICA, 1862 United States & Brazil Mail S.S. Co.
Courtesy The Peabody Museum of Salem

S.S. NORTHERN STAR, Shaw Savill Line
Courtesy Steamship Historical Society Collection, Univ. of Baltimore Library

S.S. NORWEGIAN, 1861 Allan Line
Courtesy The Peabody Museum of Salem

S.S. NOVA SCOTIA, 1926 Warren Line
Courtesy Steamship Historical Society Collection, Univ. of Baltimore Library

S.S. NOVA SCOTIAN, 1858 Allan Line
Courtesy The Peabody Museum of Salem

S.S. NUMIDIAN, 1891 Allan Line
Courtesy The Peabody Museum of Salem

S.S. NURNBERG, 1873 North German Lloyd
Courtesy The Peabody Museum of Salem

S.S. OAXACA, 1883 Compania Mexicana Transatlantica
Courtesy Alex Shaw Collection, S.S.H.S. Univ. of Baltimore Library

S.S. OBDAM, 1880 Holland American Line
Courtesy The Peabody Museum of Salem

S.S. OCEAN QUEEN, 1857 Vanderbuilt Line
Courtesy The Peabody Museum of Salem

S.S. OCEANA, 1891 Hamburg-American Line
Courtesy The Peabody Museum of Salem

S.S. OCEANIA, 1907 Austro American Line
Courtesy The Peabody Museum of Salem

S.S. OCEANIC, 1870 White Star Line
Courtesy The Peabody Museum of Salem

S.S. OCEANIC, 1870 White Star Line
Courtesy The Peabody Museum of Salem

S.S. OCEANIC, 1899 White Star Line
Courtesy The Peabody Museum of Salem

S.S. ODER, 1873 North German Lloyd
Courtesy The Peabody Museum of Salem

S.S. OHIO, 1869 North German Lloyd
Courtesy of Mystic Seaport Museum, Inc., Mystic, CT

S.S. OHIO, 1873 American Line
Courtesy The Peabody Museum of Salem

S.S. OHIO, 1923 Royal Mail Line (British)
Courtesy Henry W. Uhle Collection, S.S.H.S. Univ. of Baltimore Library

S.S. OLDENBURG, 1890 North German Lloyd
Courtesy The Peabody Museum of Salem

S.S. OLINDE RODRIGUEZ, 1873 French Line
Courtesy The Peabody Museum of Salem

S.S. OLYMPIA, 1871 Anchor Line
Courtesy The Peabody Museum of Salem

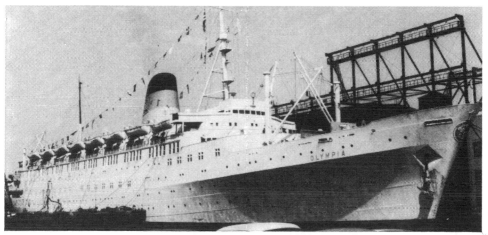

S.S. OLYMPIA, 1953 Greek Line
Courtesy Steamship Historical Society Collection, Univ. of Baltimore Library

S.S. OLYMPIC, White Star Line
Courtesy The Peabody Museum of Salem

S.S. OLYMPUS & HECLA, 1860 Cunard Line
Courtesy The Peabody Museum of Salem

S.S. ONTARIO, 1867 American S.S. Co.
Courtesy The Peabody Museum of Salem

S.S. ORANJE, 1903 Nederland Royal Mail Line
Courtesy The Peabody Museum of Salem

S.S. ORBITA, 1915 Pacific Steam Nav. Co.
Courtesy The Peabody Museum of Salem

S.S. ORCA, 1918 Royal Mail Line
Courtesy The Peabody Museum of Salem

S.S. ORDUNA, 1914 Pacific Steam Nav. Co.
Courtesy The Peabody Museum of Salem

S.S. OREGON, 1883 Dominion Line
Courtesy The Peabody Museum of Salem

S.S. OREGON, 1883 Guion Line
Courtesy The Peabody Museum of Salem

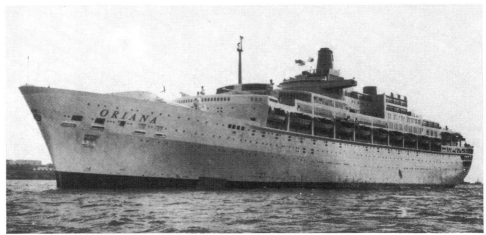

S.S. ORIANA, 1960 P & O Orient Line
Courtesy Steamship Historical Society Collection, Univ. of Baltimore Library

S.S. ORIENT, 1879 Orient Line
Courtesy The Peabody Museum of Salem

S.S. ORION, 1935 Orient Line (British)
Courtesy Steamship Historical Society Collection, Univ. of Baltimore Library

S.S. ORIONE, 1883 Italia Line
Courtesy The Peabody Museum of Salem

S.S. ORMUZ, 1886 Orient Line (British)
Courtesy The Peabody Museum of Salem

S.S. ORONSAY, 1951 Orient Line (British)
Courtesy Steamship Historical Society Collection, Univ. of Baltimore Library

S.S. ORONTES, 1902 Orient Line
Courtesy The Peabody Museum of Salem

S.S. OROPESA, 1920 Royal Mail Line (British)
Courtesy Henry W. Uhle Collection, S.S.H.S. Univ. of Baltimore Library

S.S. OROTAVA, 1889 Orient Line
Courtesy The Peabody Museum of Salem

S.S. ORSOVA, 1954 Orient Line (British)
Courtesy Steamship Historical Society Collection, Univ. of Baltimore Library

S.S. OSCAR II, 1902 Scandinavian America Line
Courtesy The Peabody Museum of Salem

S.S. OSLOFJORD, 1938 Norwegian American Line
Courtesy Steamship Historical Society Collection, Univ. of Baltimore Library

S.S. OSLOFJORD, 1949 Norwegian American Line
Courtesy Steamship Historical Society Collection, Univ. of Baltimore Library

S.S. OSTERLEY, 1909 Orient Line
Courtesy The Peabody Museum of Salem

S.S. OTRANTO, 1909 Orient Line
Courtesy The Peabody Museum of Salem

S.S. OTTAWA, 1875 Dominion Line
Courtesy The Peabody Museum of Salem

S.S. P. CALAND, 1874 Holland-American Line
Courtesy The Peabody Museum of Salem

S.S. P. DE SATRUSTEGUI, 1890 Spanish Royal Mail Line
Courtesy The Peabody Museum of Salem

S.S. PACIFIC, 1849 Collins Line
Courtesy The Peabody Museum of Salem

S.S. PALATIA, 1895 Hamburg-American Line
Courtesy The Peabody Museum of Salem

S.S. PALERMO, 1907 Italia Line
Courtesy The Peabody Museum of Salem

S.S. PALMYRA, Cunard Line
Courtesy The Peabody Museum of Salem

S.S. PANAMA, 1865 French Line
Courtesy The Peabody Museum of Salem

S.S. PANAMA, 1875 Spanish Line
Courtesy The Peabody Museum of Salem

S.S. PANNONIA, 1904 Cunard Line
Courtesy The Peabody Museum of Salem

S.S. PARIS, 1889 American Line
Courtesy The Peabody Museum of Salem

S.S. PARIS, 1921 French Line
Courtesy Steamship Historical Society Collection, Univ. of Baltimore Library

S.S. PARISIAN, 1881 Allan Line
Courtesy The Peabody Museum of Salem

S.S. PARTHIA, 1870 Cunard Line
Courtesy The Peabody Museum of Salem

S.S. PARTHIA, 1943 Cunard Line
Courtesy Steamship Historical Society Collection, Univ. of Baltimore Library

S.S. PASTEUR, 1938 Compagnie Sud Atlantique (French)
Courtesy Steamship Historical Society Collection, Univ. of Baltimore Library

S.S. PASTORES, 1912 United Fruit Co.
Courtesy The Peabody Museum of Salem

S.S. PATRIA, 1894 Hamburg-American Line
Courtesy The Peabody Museum of Salem

S.S. PATRIA, 1913 Fabre Line
Courtesy Steamship Historical Society Collection, Univ. of Baltimore Library

S.S. PATRICIA, 1902 Hamburg-American Line
Claire White Peterson Photo, Mystic Seaport, Mystic, CT

S.S. PATRICIA, 1902 Hamburg-American Line
Claire White Peterson Photo, Mystic Seaport, Mystic, CT

S.S. PATRIS, 1909 Embricos Bros.
Courtesy The Peabody Museum of Salem

S.S. PAVONIA, 1882 Cunard Line
Courtesy The Peabody Museum of Salem

S.S. PENDENNIS CASTLE, 1959 Union-Castle Line
Courtesy Steamship Historical Society Collection, Univ. of Baltimore Library

S.S. PENNLAND, 1870 Red Star-America Line
Courtesy The Peabody Museum of Salem

S.S. PENNSYLVANIA, 1863 National Line
Courtesy The Peabody Museum of Salem

S.S. PENNSYLVANIA, 1873 American Line
Courtesy The Peabody Museum of Salem

S.S. PENNSYLVANIA, 1896 Hamburg-American Line
Courtesy The Peabody Museum of Salem

S.S. PENNSYLVANIA, 1929 Panama-Pacific Line
Courtesy Steamship Historical Society Collection, Univ. of Baltimore Library

S.S. PEREIRE, 1866 French Line
Courtesy The Peabody Museum of Salem

S.S. PEROU, 1906 French Line
Courtesy The Peabody Museum of Salem

S.S. PERSEO, 1883 Italia Line
Courtesy The Peabody Museum of Salem

S.S. PERSIA, 1856 Cunard Line
Courtesy The Peabody Museum of Salem

S.S. PERUGIA, 1901 Anchor Line
Courtesy The Peabody Museum of Salem

S.S. PERUVIAN, 1863 Allan Line
Courtesy The Peabody Museum of Salem

S.S. PESARO, 1901 Italian Goverment
Courtesy The Peabody Museum of Salem

S.S. PHILADELPHIA, 1889 American Line
Courtesy The Peabody Museum of Salem

S.S. PHOENICIA, 1894 Hamburg-American Line
Courtesy The Peabody Museum of Salem

S.S. PILSUDSKI, 1935 Gdynia American Line
Courtesy Steamship Historical Society Collection, Univ. of Baltimore Library

S.S. PISA, 1896 Hamburg-American Line
Courtesy The Peabody Museum of Salem

S.S. PITTSBURG, 1922 White Star Line
Courtesy Steamship Historical Society Collection, Univ. of Baltimore Library

S.S. POCAHONTAS, 1900 United States Mail Steamship Co.
Courtesy Alex Shaw Collection, S.S.H.S. Univ. of Baltimore Library

S.S. POLAND, 1898 Atlantic Transport Line
Courtesy The Peabody Museum of Salem

S.S. POLONIA, Gdynia American Shipping Lines
Courtesy The Peabody Museum of Salem

S.S. POLYNESIAN, 1872 Allan Line
Courtesy The Peabody Museum of Salem

S.S. POMERANIAN, 1882 Allan Line
Courtesy Steamship Historical Society Collection, Univ. of Baltimore Library

S.S. POMMERANIA, 1871 Hamburg-American Line
Courtesy The Peabody Museum of Salem

S.S. PRESIDENT ARTHUR, 1900 Hamburg-American Line
Courtesy The Peabody Museum of Salem

S.S. PRESIDENT FILLMORE, 1899 United States Line
Courtesy The Peabody Museum of Salem

S.S. PRESIDENT GRANT, 1900 United States Line
Courtesy of Mystic Seaport Museum, Inc., Mystic, CT

S.S. PRESIDENT LINCOLN, 1907 Hamburg-American Line
Courtesy The Peabody Museum of Salem

S.S. PRESIDENT MONROE, 1920 United States Line
Courtesy Steamship Historical Society Collection, Univ. of Baltimore Library

S.S. PRESIDENT POLK, 1921 United States Line
Courtesy Alex Shaw Collection, S.S.H.S. Univ. of Baltimore Library

S.S. PRESIDENT ROOSEVELT, 1922 United States Line
Courtesy Steamship Historical Society Collection, Univ. of Baltimore Library

S.S. PRESIDENT TAFT, 1921 Dollar Steamship Line
Courtesy Steamship Historical Society Collection, Univ. of Baltimore Library

S.S. PRESIDENT VAN BUREN, 1920 United States Line
Courtesy Steamship Historical Society Collection, Univ. of Baltimore Library

S.S. PRESIDENT WILSON, 1948 Dollar Steamship Line
Courtesy Steamship Historical Society Collection, Univ. of Baltimore Library

S.S. PRESIDENTE WILSON, 1912 Austro-American Line
Courtesy The Peabody Museum of Salem

S.S. PRETORIA, 1897 Hamburg-American Line
Courtesy Steamship Historical Society Collection, Univ. of Baltimore Library

S.S. PRETORIAN, 1900 Allan Line
Courtesy The Peabody Museum of Salem

S.S. PREUSSEN, 1886 North German Lloyd
Courtesy The Peabody Museum of Salem

S.S. PRINCE GEORGE, 1898
Courtesy Steamship Historical Society Collection, Univ. of Baltimore Library

S.S. PRINCE GEORGE, 1910
Courtesy Steamship Historical Society Collection, Univ. of Baltimore Library

S.S. PRINCEPESSA YOLANDA, 1907 Lloyd Italiana
Courtesy The Peabody Museum of Salem

S.S. PRINCESS HELENE, 1930
Courtesy Steamship Historical Society Collection, Univ. of Baltimore Library

S.S. PRINCESS MARGUERITE, 1949
Courtesy Steamship Historical Society Collection, Univ. of Baltimore Library

S.S. PRINCESS MATOIKA, 1900 United States Mail Steamship Co.
Courtesy Steamship Historical Society Collection, Univ. of Baltimore Library

S.S. PRINCIPE DE PIEMONTE, 1907 Lloyd Sabaudo
Courtesy The Peabody Museum of Salem

S.S. PRINCIPE DE UDINE, 1908 Lloyd Sabaudo
Courtesy The Peabody Museum of Salem

S.S. PRINCIPE UMBERTO, 1909 Italia Line
Courtesy The Peabody Museum of Salem

S.S. PRINCIPELLO, 1907 Uranium S.S. Co.
Courtesy The Peabody Museum of Salem

S.S. PRINZ ADALBERT, 1902 Hamburg-American Line
Courtesy The Peabody Museum of Salem

S.S. PRINZ EITEL FRIEDRICH, 1904 North German Lloyd
Courtesy The Peabody Museum of Salem

S.S. PRINZ FRIEDRICH WILHELM, 1907 North German Lloyd
Courtesy The Peabody Museum of Salem

S.S. PRINZ OSKAR, 1902 Hamburg American Line
Courtesy The Peabody Museum of Salem

S.S. PRINZ SISISMOND, 1903 Hamburg-American Line
Courtesy The Peabody Museum of Salem

S.S. PRINZESS ALICE, 1900 North German Lloyd
Courtesy Steamship Historical Society Collection, Univ. of Baltimore Library

S.S. PRINZESS IRENE, 1900 North German Lloyd
Courtesy The Peabody Museum of Salem

S.S. PRINZESSIN VICTORIA LUISE, 1900 Hamburg-American Line
Courtesy The Peabody Museum of Salem

S.S. PROVENCE, 1906 French Line
Courtesy The Peabody Museum of Salem

S.S. PROVIDENCE, 1915 Fabre Line
Courtesy The Peabody Museum of Salem

S.S. PRUSSIA, Hamburg-American Line
Courtesy The Peabody Museum of Salem

S.S. PUERTO RICO, 1913 French Line
Courtesy Henry W. Uhle Collection, S.S.H.S. Univ. of Baltimore Library

S.S. PULASKI, 1912 Gdynia American Line
Courtesy Steamship Historical Society Collection, Univ. of Baltimore Library

S.S. QUAKER CITY, 1867 North German Lloyd
Courtesy Steamship Historical Society Collection, Univ. of Baltimore Library

S.S. QUEBEC, 1896 French Line
Courtesy The Peabody Museum of Salem

S.S. QUEEN ELIZABETH, 1940 Cunard Line
Courtesy Steamship Historical Society Collection, Univ. of Baltimore Library

S.S. QUEEN MARY, 1935 Cunard Line
Courtesy Steamship Historical Society Collection, Univ. of Baltimore Library

S.S. RE D'ITALIA, 1907 Italia Line
Courtesy The Peabody Museum of Salem

S.S. REGINA, 1918 Dominion Line
Courtesy The Peabody Museum of Salem

S.S. REGINA D'ITALAIA, 1907 Lloyd Sabando
Courtesy The Peabody Museum of Salem

S.S. REGINA ELENA, 1907 Italia Line
Courtesy The Peabody Museum of Salem

S.S. REGINA MARGHERITA, 1884 Italia Line
Courtesy The Peabody Museum of Salem

S.S. REINA DEL MAR, Italia Line
Courtesy Steamship Historical Society Collection, Univ. of Baltimore Library

S.S. REINA MARIA CHRISTINA, 1888 Spanish Line
Courtesy The Peabody Museum of Salem

S.S. RELIANCE, 1920 Hamburg American Line
Courtesy Steamship Historical Society Collection, Univ. of Baltimore Library

S.S. REPUBLIC, 1871 White Star Line
Courtesy The Peabody Museum of Salem

S.S. REPUBLIC II, 1903 White Star Line
Courtesy The Peabody Museum of Salem

S.S. REPUBLIC, 1907 United States Line
Courtesy The Peabody Museum of Salem

S.S. RESOLUTE, 1920 Hamburg-American Line
Courtesy Steamship Historical Society Collection, Univ. of Baltimore Library

S.S. RE VITTORIO, 1907 Italia Line
Courtesy The Peabody Museum of Salem

S.S. REX, 1932 Italia Line
Courtesy Steamship Historical Society Collection, Univ. of Baltimore Library

S.S. RHAETIA, 1883 Hamburg-American Line
Courtesy The Peabody Museum of Salem

S.S. RHAETIA II, 1905 Hamburg-American Line
Courtesy The Peabody Museum of Salem

S.S. RHEIN, 1899 North German Lloyd
Courtesy The Peabody Museum of Salem

S.S. RHYNLAND I, 1878 Red Star-American Line
Courtesy The Peabody Museum of Salem

S.S. RIJNDAM, 1901 Holland American Line
Courtesy Steamship Historical Society Collection, Univ. of Baltimore Library

S.S. ROCHAMBEAU, 1911 French Line
Courtesy Steamship Historical Society Collection, Univ. of Baltimore Library

S.S. ROMA, 1901 Fabre Line
Courtesy The Peabody Museum of Salem

S.S. ROMA, 1926 Italia Line
Courtesy Steamship Historical Society Collection, Univ. of Baltimore Library

S.S. ROMANIC, 1898 White Star Line
Courtesy The Peabody Museum of Salem

S.S. ROON, 1903 North German Lloyd
Courtesy of Mystic Seaport Museum, Inc., Mystic, CT

S.S. ROSARIAN, 1887 Allan Line
Courtesy The Peabody Museum of Salem

S.S. ROSLIN CASTLE, 1883 Union-Castle Line
Courtesy Steamship Historical Society Collection, Univ. of Baltimore Library

S.S. ROTTERDAM, 1872 Holland America Line
Courtesy The Peabody Museum of Salem

S.S. ROTTERDAM II, 1878 Holland America Line
Courtesy The Peabody Museum of Salem

S.S. ROTTERDAM III, 1897 Holland America Line
Courtesy The Peabody Museum of Salem

S.S. ROTTERDAM, 1908 Holland America Line
Courtesy The Peabody Museum of Salem

S.S. ROTTERDAM, 1959 Holland America Line
Courtesy Steamship Historical Society Collection, Univ. of Baltimore Library

S.S. ROUSSILLON, 1906 French Line
Courtesy The Peabody Museum of Salem

S.S. ROYAL EDWARD, 1908 Canadian Northern S.S. Co.
Courtesy The Peabody Museum of Salem

S.S. ROYAL GEORGE, 1907 Canadian Northern S.S. Co.
Courtesy The Peabody Museum of Salem

S.S. RUGIA, 1882 Hamburg-American Line
Courtesy Steamship Historical Society Collection, Univ. of Baltimore Library

S.S. RUGIA II, 1905 Hamburg-American Line
Courtesy The Peabody Museum of Salem

S.S. RUNIC, 1899 White Star Line
Courtesy The Peabody Museum of Salem

S.S. RUSSIA, 1867 Cunard Line
Courtesy Steamship Historical Society Collection, Univ. of Baltimore Library

S.S. RUSSIA, 1889 Hamburg-American Line
Courtesy The Peabody Museum of Salem

S.S. RYNDAM, 1951 Holland-American Line
Courtesy The Peabody Museum of Salem

S.S. SAALE, 1886 North German Lloyd
Courtesy of Mystic Seaport Museum, Inc., Mystic, CT

S.S. SACHEM, 1893 Warren Line
Courtesy The Peabody Museum of Salem

S.S. SACHSEN, 1886 North German Lloyd
Courtesy The Peabody Museum of Salem

S.S. SAGAMORE, 1892 Warren Line
Courtesy The Peabody Museum of Salem

S.S. SAINT GERMAIN, 1874 French Line
Courtesy The Peabody Museum of Salem

S.S. ST. LAURENT, 1866 French Line
Courtesy The Peabody Museum of Salem

S.S. ST. LOUIS, 1895 American Line
Courtesy Steamship Historical Society Collection, Univ. of Baltimore Library

S.S. ST. LOUIS, 1929 Hamburg-American Line
Courtesy Steamship Historical Society Collection, Univ. of Baltimore Library

S.S. ST. PAUL, 1895 American Line
Courtesy Steamship Historical Society Collection, Univ. of Baltimore Library

S.S. SAINT SIMON, 1874 French Line
Courtesy The Peabody Museum of Salem

S.S. SALIER, 1875 North German Lloyd
Courtesy The Peabody Museum of Salem

S.S. SAMARIA, 1868 Cunard Line
Courtesy The Peabody Museum of Salem

S.S. SAMLAND, 1903 Red Star Line
Courtesy The Peabody Museum of Salem

S.S. SAN GIORGIO, 1886 Sicilia Americana Line
Courtesy The Peabody Museum of Salem

S.S. SAN GIORGIO, 1907 Pcircc Bros.
Courtesy The Peabody Museum of Salem

S.S. SAN GUGLIELMO, 1911 Pierce Bros.
Courtesy The Peabody Museum of Salem

S.S. SANNIO, 1899 Italia Line
Courtesy The Peabody Museum of Salem

S.S. SANTA ANNA, 1910 Fabre Line
Courtesy The Peabody Museum of Salem

S.S. SANTA INEZ, 1929 Grace Line
Courtesy Steamship Historical Society Collection, Univ. of Baltimore Library

S.S. SANTA MARIA, 1928 Grace Line
Courtesy Steamship Historical Society Collection, Univ. of Baltimore Library

S.S. SANTA RITA, 1929 Grace S.S. Co., Inc.
Courtesy The Peabody Museum of Salem

S.S. SANTA ROSA, 1932 Grace Line
Courtesy Steamship Historical Society Collection, Univ. of Baltimore Library

S.S. SARAGOSSA, 1874 Cunard Line
Courtesy The Peabody Museum of Salem

S.S. SARDEGNA, 1902 Navigazione Generale Italiana
Courtesy The Peabody Museum of Salem

S.S. SARDINIAN, 1875 Allan Line
Courtesy The Peabody Museum of Salem

S.S. SARMATIAN, 1871 Allan Line
Courtesy The Peabody Museum of Salem

S.S. SARNIA, 1882 Dominion Line
Courtesy The Peabody Museum of Salem

S.S. SATURNIA, 1910 Anchor Donaldson Line
Courtesy The Peabody Museum of Salem

S.S. SATURNIA, 1927 Italia Line
Courtesy Steamship Historical Society Collection, Univ. of Baltimore Library

S.S. SAVANNAH, 1819 Col. John Stevens (U.S.)
Courtesy The Peabody Museum of Salem

S.S. SAVOIA, 1897 La Veloce
Courtesy The Peabody Museum of Salem

S.S. SAXONIA, 1857 Hamburg-American Line
Courtesy The Peabody Museum of Salem

Souvenir Plate, S.S. SAXONIA, 1900 Cunard Line
Courtesy of Henry and Barbara Hoffmann, Menominee, MI

S.S. SAXONIA, 1900 Cunard Line
Courtesy The Peabody Museum of Salem

S.S. SAXONIA, 1954 Cunard Line
Courtesy Steamship Historical Society Collection, Univ. of Baltimore Library

S.S. SCANDIA, 1889 Hamburg-American Line
Courtesy The Peabody Museum of Salem

S.S. SCANDINAVIAN, 1870 Allan Line
Courtesy The Peabody Museum of Salem

S.S. SCANDINAVIAN, 1898 Canadian Pacific Steamships
Courtesy The Peabody Museum of Salem

S.S. SCANMAIL, 1919 American Scantic Line
Courtesy Steamship Historical Society Collection, Univ. of Baltimore Library

S.S. SCHARNHORST, 1904 Norddeutscher Lloyd
Courtesy The Peabody Museum of Salem

S.S. SCHILLER, 1873 Eagle Line
Courtesy The Peabody Museum of Salem

S.S. SCHLESWIG, 1903 North German Lloyd
Courtesy The Peabody Museum of Salem

S.S. SCOTIA, 1862 Cunard Line
Courtesy of Mystic Seaport Museum, Inc., Mystic, CT

S.S. SCOTIA, 1862 Cunard Line
Courtesy The Peabody Museum of Salem

S.S. SCOTIA, 1889 Hamburg-American Line
Courtesy The Peabody Museum of Salem

S.S. SCOTIAN, 1898 Allan Line
Courtesy The Peabody Museum of Salem

S.S. SCOTSMAN, 1899 Dominion Line
Courtesy The Peabody Museum of Salem

S.S. SCYTHIA I, 1875 Cunard Line
Courtesy The Peabody Museum of Salem

S.S. SCYTHIA, 1920 Cunard Line
Courtesy Steamship Historical Society Collection, Univ. of Baltimore Library

S.S. SERVIA, 1881 Cunard Line
Courtesy Steamship Historical Society Collection, Univ. of Baltimore Library

S.S. SEVEN SEAS, 1940 Europe Canada Line (German)
Courtesy Alex Shaw Collection, S.S.H.S. Univ. of Baltimore Library

S.S. SEYDLITZ, 1902 North German Lloyd
Courtesy The Peabody Museum of Salem

S.S. SIBERIA, 1867 Cunard Line
Courtesy The Peabody Museum of Salem

S.S. SICILIAN, 1899 Allan Line
Courtesy The Peabody Museum of Salem

S.S. SICILIAN PRINCE, 1889 Prince Line Ltd.
Courtesy The Peabody Museum of Salem

S.S. SIERRA, 1900 Oceanic Steamship Co.
Courtesy The Peabody Museum of Salem

S.S. SIERRA, 1928
Courtesy Steamship Historical Society Collection, Univ. of Baltimore Library

S.S. SIERRA VENTANA, 1923 North German Lloyd
Courtesy Alex Shaw Collection, S.S.H.S. Univ. of Baltimore Library

S.S. SILESIA I, 1869 Hamburg-American Line
Courtesy The Peabody Museum of Salem

S.S. SLAVOINA, 1903 Cunard Line
Courtesy Alex Shaw Collection, S.S.H.S. Univ. of Baltimore Library

S.S. SMOLENSK, 1901 Russian Volunteer Fleet
Courtesy Steamship Historical Society Collection, Univ. of Baltimore Library

S.S. SOBIESKI, 1939 Gdynia American Line
Courtesy Steamship Historical Society Collection, Univ. of Baltimore Library

S.S. SOUTHWARK, 1893 American Line
Courtesy The Peabody Museum of Salem

S.S. SPAARNDAM, 1922 Holland America Line
Courtesy of Mystic Seaport Museum, Inc., Mystic, CT

S.S. SPAIN, 1871 National Line
Courtesy The Peabody Museum of Salem

S.S. SPREE, 1890 North German Lloyd
Courtesy The Peabody Museum of Salem

S.S. STAMPALIA, 1909 Le Veloce Line
Courtesy Alex Shaw Collection, S.S.H.S. Univ. of Baltimore Library

S.S. STATE OF CALIFORNIA, 1891 Allan Line
Courtesy Alex Shaw Collection, S.S.H.S. Univ. of Baltimore Library

S.S. STATE OF INDIANA, 1874 State Steamship Co., Ltd.
Courtesy The Peabody Museum of Salem

S.S. STATE OF NEBRASKA, 1880 State Line (British)
Courtesy The Peabody Museum of Salem

S.S. STATE OF NEVADA, 1874 State Steamship Co., Ltd.
Courtesy The Peabody Museum of Salem

S.S. STATE OF PENNSYLVANIA, 1873 State Line
Courtesy The Peabody Museum of Salem

S.S. STATENDAM, 1898 Holland America Line
Courtesy The Peabody Museum of Salem

S.S. STATENDAM, 1929 Holland America Line
Courtesy Steamship Historical Society Collection, Univ. of Baltimore Library

S.S. STATENDAM, 1957 Holland America Line
Courtesy Steamship Historical Society Collection, Univ. of Baltimore Library

S.S. STIRLINGCASTLE, 1936 Union Castle Mail S.S. Co.
Courtesy of Mystic Seaport Museum, Inc., Mystic, CT

S.S. STOCKHOLM, 1900 Swedish American Line
Courtesy The Peabody Museum of Salem

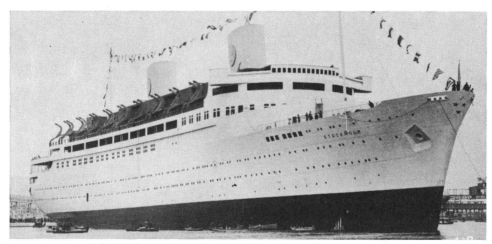

S.S. STOCKHOLM, 1940 Swedish American Line
Courtesy Steamship Historical Society Collection, Univ. of Baltimore Library

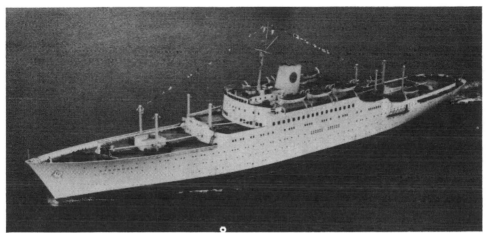

S.S. STOCKHOLM, 1947 Swedish American Line
Courtesy Steamship Historical Society Collection, Univ. of Baltimore Library

S.S. STRASSBURG, 1872 North German Lloyd
Courtesy The Peabody Museum of Salem

S.S. STUTTGART, 1889 North German Lloyd
Courtesy The Peabody Museum of Salem

S.S. SUEVIA, 1874 Hamburg-American Line
Courtesy Steamship Historical Society Collection, Univ. of Baltimore Library

S.S. SUFFREN, 1901 French Line
Courtesy The Peabody Museum of Salem

S.S. SUSQUEHANNA, 1899 U.S. Mail S.S. Co.
Courtesy The Peabody Museum of Salem

S.S. SWITZERLAND, 1874 Red Star-American Line
Courtesy The Peabody Museum of Salem

S.S. TAORMINA, 1908 Lloyd Italiano
Courtesy Steamship Historical Society Collection, Univ. of Baltimore Library

S.S. TARSUS, 1931 Turkish State Maritime
Courtesy Alex Shaw Collection, S.S.H.S. Univ. of Baltimore Library

S.S. TENNYSON, 1900 Lamport & Holt, Ltd.
Courtesy The Peabody Museum of Salem

S.S. TERESA, 1900 Unione Austneco
Courtesy The Peabody Museum of Salem

S.S. TEUTONIA, 1856, Hamburg-American Line
Courtesy The Peabody Museum of Salem

S.S. TEUTONIC, 1889 White Star Line
Courtesy The Peabody Museum of Salem

S.S. THAMES, 1890 Royal Mail Line
Courtesy The Peabody Museum of Salem

S.S. THE QUEEN, 1864 National Line (British)
Courtesy Steamship Historical Society Collection, Univ. of Baltimore Library

S.S. THINGVALLA, 1874 Thingvalla Line
Courtesy The Peabody Museum of Salem

S.S. THURINGIA, 1922 Hamburg-American Line
Courtesy of Mystic Seaport Museum, Inc., Mystic, CT

S.S. TIGRE, 1862 French Line
Courtesy The Peabody Museum of Salem

S.S. TINTAGEL CASTLE, 1896 Castle Line
Courtesy The Peabody Museum of Salem

S.S. TIRPITZ I, 1914 Hamburg-American Line
Courtesy The Peabody Museum of Salem

S.S. TITANIC, 1911 White Star Line
Courtesy The Peabody Museum of Salem

S.S. TOLOA, 1917 United Fruit Co.
Courtesy Steamship Historical Society Collection, Univ. of Baltimore Library

S.S. TOLOA, 1917 United Fruit Co.
Courtesy The Peabody Museum of Salem

S.S. TOMASO DI SAVOIA, 1907 Lloyd Sabaudo
Courtesy The Peabody Museum of Salem

S.S. TORONTO, 1880 Dominion Line
Courtesy The Peabody Museum of Salem

S.S. TORTONA, 1909 Cairns Noble & Co., Ltd.
Courtesy The Peabody Museum of Salem

S.S. TRANSVAAL CASTLE, 1961 Union Castle Line
Courtesy The Peabody Museum of Salem

S.S. TRANSYLVANIA, 1914 Cunard Line
Courtesy The Peabody Museum of Salem

S.S. TRAVE, 1866 North German Lloyd
Courtesy of Mystic Seaport Museum, Inc., Mystic, CT

S.S. TRENT, 1900 Royal Mail Line
Courtesy The Peabody Museum of Salem

S.S. TRINACRIA, 1871 Anchor Line
Courtesy The Peabody Museum of Salem

S.S. TRIPOLI, 1863 Cunard Line
Courtesy The Peabody Museum of Salem

S.S. TUNISIAN, 1900 Allan Line
Courtesy The Peabody Museum of Salem

S.S. TUSCANIA, 1914 Anchor Line
Courtesy The Peabody Museum of Salem

S.S. ULTONIA, 1826 Cunard Line
Courtesy The Peabody Museum of Salem

S.S. UMBRIA, 1884 Cunard Line
Courtesy of Mystic Seaport Museum, Inc., Mystic, CT

S.S. UNITED STATES, 1903 Scandinavian American Line
Courtesy The Peabody Museum of Salem

S.S. UNITED STATES, 1952
Courtesy Steamship Historical Society Collection, Univ. of Baltimore Library

S.S. UTOPIA, 1874 Anchor Line
Courtesy The Peabody Museum of Salem

S.S. VADERLAND, 1873 Red Star Line
Courtesy The Peabody Museum of Salem

S.S. VANCOUVER, 1884 Dominion Line
Courtesy The Peabody Museum of Salem

S.S. VANDALIA, 1870 Hamburg-American Line
Courtesy The Peabody Museum of Salem

S.S. VANDERBILT, 1855 Vanderbilt Line
Courtesy The Peabody Museum of Salem

S.S. VASCO NUNEZ DE BALBOA, 1891 Spanish Royal Mail Line
Courtesy The Peabody Museum of Salem

S.S. VASCONIA, 1899 Cypriene Fabre
Courtesy The Peabody Museum of Salem

S.S. VATERLAND, 1914 Hamburg American Line
Courtesy Steamship Historical Society Collection, Univ. of Baltimore Library

S.S. VATERLAND, 1940 Hamburg-American Line
Courtesy The Peabody Museum of Salem

S.S. VEDIC, 1918 White Star Line
Courtesy Alex Shaw Collection, S.S.H.S. Univ. of Baltimore Library

S.S. VEENDAM, 1871 Holland America Line
Courtesy The Peabody Museum of Salem

S.S. VENEZIA, 1907 Cyprien Fabre Line
Courtesy The Peabody Museum of Salem

S.S. VENEZUELA, 1906 Royal Netherlands S.S. Co.
Courtesy The Peabody Museum of Salem

S.S. VENTURA, 1900 Oceanic Steamship Co.
Courtesy The Peabody Museum of Salem

S.S. VERONA, 1908 Italia Line
Courtesy The Peabody Museum of Salem

S.S. VICKSBURG, 1872 Dominion Line
Courtesy The Peabody Museum of Salem

S.S. VICTORIA I, 1872 Anchor Line
Courtesy The Peabody Museum of Salem

S.S. VICTORIA, 1931 Lloyd Triestino Line
Courtesy Steamship Historical Society Collection, Univ. of Baltimore Library

S.S. VICTORIA LUISE, 1899 Hamburg-American Line
Courtesy Steamship Historical Society Collection, Univ. of Baltimore Library

S.S. VICTORIAN, 1895 F. Leyland & Co.
Courtesy The Peabody Museum of Salem

S.S. VICTORIAN, 1904 Allan Line
Courtesy The Peabody Museum of Salem

S.S. VILLE DE BORDEAUX, 1870 French Line
Courtesy The Peabody Museum of Salem

S.S. VILLE DE BREST, 1870 French Line
Courtesy The Peabody Museum of Salem

S.S. VILLE DE MARSEILLE, 1874 French Line
Courtesy The Peabody Museum of Salem

S.S. VILLE DE PARIS, 1866 French Line
Courtesy The Peabody Museum of Salem

S.S. VILLE DE ST. NAZAIRE, 1870 French Line
Courtesy The Peabody Museum of Salem

S.S. VILLE DU HAVRE, 1866 French Line
Courtesy The Peabody Museum of Salem

S.S. VIRGINIAN, 1905 Allan Line
Courtesy The Peabody Museum of Salem

S.S. VLADIMIR, 1895 Russian Volunteer Fleet
Courtesy The Peabody Museum of Salem

S.S. VOLENDAM, 1922 Holland American Line
Courtesy The Peabody Museum of Salem

S.S. VULCANIA, 1928 Italia Line
Courtesy Steamship Historical Society Collection, Univ. of Baltimore Library

S.S. WAESLAND, 1867, Red Star-American Line
Courtesy The Peabody Museum of Salem

S.S. WALDENSIAN, 1861 Allan Line
Courtesy The Peabody Museum of Salem

S.S. WASHINGTON, 1864 French Linc
Courtesy The Peabody Museum of Salem

S.S. WASHINGTON, 1880 La Veluce
Courtesy The Peabody Museum of Salem

S.S. WASHINGTON, 1933 U.S. LINES
Courtesy Steamship Historical Society Collection, Univ. of Baltimore Library

S.S. WEIMAR, 1891 North German Lloyd
Courtesy The Peabody Museum of Salem

S.S. WERKENDAM, 1882 Holland America Line
Courtesy The Peabody Museum of Salem

S.S. WERRA, 1882 North German Lloyd
Courtesy of Mystic Seaport Museum, Inc., Mystic, CT

S.S. WESTERNLAND, 1884 Red Star Line
Courtesy of Mystic Seaport Museum, Inc., Mystic, CT

S.S. WESTERNLAND, 1918 Red Star Line
Courtesy of Mystic Seaport Museum, Inc., Mystic, CT

S.S. WESTPHALIA, 1868 Hamburg American Line
Courtesy Steamship Historical Society Collection, Univ. of Baltimore Library

S.S. WESTPHALIA, 1923 Hamburg American Line
Courtesy Steamship Historical Society Collection, Univ. of Baltimore Library

S.S. WIELAND, 1874 Hamburg-American Line
Courtesy The Peabody Museum of Salem

S.S. WILHELMINA, 1909 Matson Line
Courtesy The Peabody Museum of Salem

S.S. WILLEHAD, 1894 North German Lloyd
Courtesy The Peabody Museum of Salem

S.S. WILLEM RUYS, 1947 Rotterdam Lloyd
Courtesy Steamship Historical Society Collection, Univ. of Baltimore Library

S.S. WINCHESTER CASTLE, 1930 Union Castle Mail S.S. Co.
Courtesy The Peabody Museum of Salem

S.S. WINIFREDIAN, 1899 Leyland Line (British)
Courtesy Steamship Historical Society Collection, Univ. of Baltimore Library

S.S. WINNIPEG, 1918 French Line
Courtesy Henry W. Uhle Collection, S.S.H.S. Univ. of Baltimore Library

S.S. WISCONSIN, 1870 Guion Line
Courtesy The Peabody Museum of Salem

S.S. WITTEKIND, North German Lloyd
Courtesy The Peabody Museum of Salem

S.S. WYOMING, 1870 Guion Line
Courtesy The Peabody Museum of Salem

S.S. YORCK, 1906 North German Lloyd
Courtesy The Peabody Museum of Salem

S.S. YORKSHIRE, 1889 Bibby Bros. & Co.
Courtesy The Peabody Museum of Salem

S.S. YPIRANGA, 1908 Hamburg-American Line
Courtesy The Peabody Museum of Salem

S.S. ZAANDAM, 1882 Holland America Line
Courtesy The Peabody Museum of Salem

S.S. ZAANDAM, 1939 Holland America Line
Courtesy Everett E. Viez Collection, S.S.H.S. Univ. of Baltimore Library

S.S. ZEELAND, 1901 Red Star Line
Courtesy The Peabody Museum of Salem

S.S. ZEPPELIN, 1914 North German Lloyd
Courtesy Steamship Historical Society Collection, Univ. of Baltimore Library

S.S. ZIETEN, 1902 North German Lloyd
Courtesy Steamship Historical Society Collection, Univ. of Baltimore Library

S.S. ZION, 1956 Zim Israel Navigation Co.
Courtesy Everett E. Viez Collection, S.S.H.S. Univ. of Baltimore Library

S.S. ZUIDERKRUIS, 1944 Holland American Line
Courtesy Steamship Historical Society Collection, Univ. of Baltimore Library

STEAMSHIP LINES

In the course of more than one hundred years there were well over two hundred major steamship lines operating fleets of ships on the oceans of the world. Some of the lines owned and operated only a few ships while some of the major lines operated well over 150 ships. Some lines confined themselves to the Atlantic, while others plied the Pacific and Indian Ocean. Some ships were operated in Round-the-World cruises.

From the European ports, ships were operated overseas by nearly all of the maritime nations. Starting in the north Atlantic, the Norwegian, Swedish, Finnish, Baltic, Polish, Russian, Danish, Nederlands, British, Belgian, French, Spanish, Italian, Greek, Turkish and Israel nations were represented.

When the change came from sail to steam, paddle-wheels (side-wheelers) were first used for propulsion, but in a short time all were converted to propellers or screws. At first only a single propeller was used. As ships became longer and larger, the number of propellers increased to two, three and finally four in the case of the largest ships such as the Queen Elizabeth and Queen Mary. The longest ships were the FRANCE, 1035 feet, QUEEN ELIZABETH, 1031 feet, NORMANDIE, 1027 feet, QUEEN MARY, 1018 feet, and, the UNITED STATES 990 feet.

Speed of travel on the ocean was one of the most important factors in attracting passenger traffic. A land mile is 5,280 feet whereas a nautical mile (sea-level) is 6,080 feet. Thus, ten knots of ocean travel equals 11.515 miles per hour; 20 knots 23.03 miles per hour. The distance between Liverpool and New York is 3058 miles; New York and Hamburg, 3536 miles; Bremen 3590 miles; New York and Goteborg, Sweden 3738 miles. Crossing between ports in the shortest time was most important.

In researching for pictures of ships, a few post card pictures sold at ports or on shipboard were found. These were in the nature of souvenirs of the voyage. These postal cards were in color and were cherished by those who obtained them for many years. The following ten pages of post card pictures illustrate the competitive spirit among the steamship lines for passenger business.

RED STAR LINE Mail Steamers sailed every Saturday between New York and Antwerp and every third week between Philadelphia and Antwerp. The WESTERNLAND (5,550 tons) was the largest RED STAR LINE steamship when this card was issued in the 1880's.

The RED STAR LINE steamships served New York and Philadelphia every week in the 1880's. Their ships had their names end with "Land." The RED STAR LINE served into the 20th century and was a sister company of the WHITE STAR LINE.

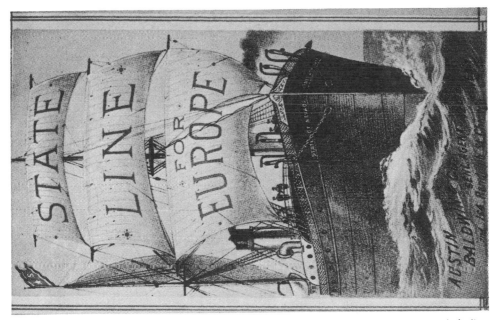

The NORTH GERMAN LLOYD'S
S.S. FULDA was 4,816 tons, 438 feet
long, 46 feet wide, single-screw, iron
hulled and 17 knots. She carried 125
First Class, 130 Second Class and
1,000 Third Class passengers. Her
maiden voyage was Bremen-South-
Hampton-New York, March 12,
1883. Sister ship: WERRA.

The STATE LINE was a transatlantic
steamship company during the latter
years of the 19th century. Their ships
were named after states in America.

STATE LINE steamers were named after states in the United States. These fine ships served from New York to Glasgow, Liverpool and Belfast. A First Cabin Single Berth cost $60 to $75 in the 1880's. A Second Cabin Berth was $40.

The KAISER WILHELM II, a NORTH GERMAN LLOYD steamship, was 449 feet long, 51 feet wide, 4,773 tons, single-screw, and 16 knots. She was launched April 23, 1889. She carried 120 First Class, 80 Second Class and 1,000 Third Class passengers. She was wrecked in 1908.

The STATE LINE had their ships named after states in the United States. This very rare dock view of the STATE STEAM SHIP CO. on sailing day gives an idea of the activity with steamship travel in the 1880's.

The GUION LINE steamship ARIZONA was the Atlantic speed record holder in the 1880's. The ARIZONA survided a head-on collision with an iceberg off the Grand Banks. Her smashed in bow was repaired with a wooden one at St. John's, Newfoundland. She then raced back to Liverpool in 6 days, 17 hours and 30 minutes. No one was lost in the accident.

The INMAN STEAMSHIP COMPANY operated what many call "the most beautiful ships": the CITY OF NEW YORK AND CITY OF PARIS. They were the first ships with twin screws. These ships later became part of the AMERICAN LINE.

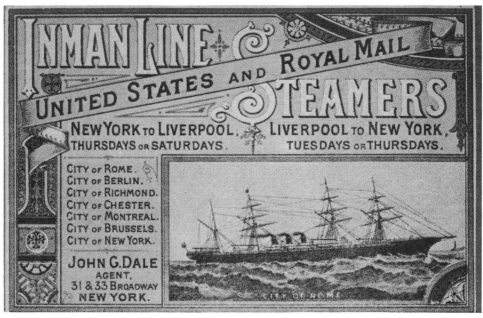

THE CITY OF ROME is considered by many nautical historians to have been the most beautiful 19th century steamship. Her maiden voyage in October, 1881, proved slow and her engines were overhauled. She was 560 feet long with beautiful interiors. The INMAN LINE later sold her to the ANCHOR LINE.

The NATIONAL LINE's S.S. EGYPT was 5,089 tons, 440 feet long, 43 feet wide, single-screw, 12½ knots and launched February 9, 1871. Saloon passage ranged from $50. to $70. and Steerage only $26. from Great Britain.

The NATIONAL LINE Operated 13 steamships in the 1880's with the S.S. AMERICA being the largest at 6,000 tons and the fastest. She entered service in 1884.

The SERVIA was the first steel CUNARD Liner and also had the first electric lights. At 7,400 tons with 10,500 horse power engines, she could steam 16½ knots.

The CUNARD steamships ETRURIA and sistership UMBRIA were launched in 1884. Each was 500 feet long with a gross tonnage of 8,127 tons. With engines that could produce 14,500 horse-power, they could steam at 19½ knots. They carried 550 First Class passengers and 800 emigrants.

The WHITE STAR LINE was a major steamship company from the 1870's through to 1934 when it merged with the Cunard Steamship Company Limited. The ship depicted is the BRITANNIC (1874).

The GERMANIC, a WHITE STAR LINE steamship, was 455 feet long, 45 feet wide, iron hulled, with a single-screw and steamed 16 knots. Her maiden voyage was May 20, 1875 and won the transatlantic "Blue Ribbon" in February, 1876. Long lived, the GERMANIC was scrapped in 1950. Her sister ship was the BRITANNIC. Both carried 220 First Class and 900 Third Class passengers.

This TITANIC post card is like those mailed on her maiden voyage April 10, 1912. She struck an iceberg on April 14th and sank at 2:20 a.m. the next morning. Over 1500 people perished.

This view of the OLYMPIC (larger) and TITANIC is from an original steamship office picture which hung for display to help with ticket sales. It is the only known view of the ships together in a painting.

The ALLAN LINE introduced the first steel ship, the BUENOS AYREAN, in 1881, just before the CUNARD LINE steamship SERVIA entered service. The ALLAN LINE served passengers mainly to Canada and the United States well into the 20th century bringing about many dramatic innovations.

BIBLIOGRAPHY

AMERICAN HISTORICAL SOCIETY OF GERMANS FROM RUSSIA, "Clues", Lincoln, Nebraska

AMERICAN HISTORICAL SOCIETY OF GERMANS FROM RUSSIA, "Journal", Lincoln, Nebraska

ANDERSON, ROY "White Star", T. Stephenson & Sons Ltd., Prescot, Lancashire, 1964

ANGAS, COMMANDER W. MACK, "Rivalry on the Atlantic 1883-1939" Lee Furman, New York, 1939

APPLEYARD, ROLLO, "Charles Parsons: His Life and Work" Constable & Co., Ltd., London 1933.

ARMSTRONG, WARREN, "Atlantic Highway", Johy Day Company, New York, 1962

ALYMER, GERALD, "R.M.S. Mauretania; The Ship and Her Record" P. Marshall & Co., Ltd., London 1934

BABCOCK, F. LAWRENCE "Spanning the Atlantic" Alfred A. Knopf, New York, 1931

BAKER, GEORGE S. "Ship form, Resistance and Screw Propulsion" D. Van Nostrand Co. New York, 1915.

BARBANCE, MARTHE, "Histoire de la Compagnie Generale Transatlantique" Arts et Meitiers Graphiques, Paris, 1955.

BARNABY K.C., "Some Ship Disasters and Their Causes"

BATE, GEORGE W. "Transatlantic Observation" Wisconsin Magazine of History, 1981

BEAUDIN, RAOUL DE "Captain of the Ile" translated by Salvator Attanasio, McGraw-Hill Book Company, New York, 1960.

BEAUDEAN, RAOUL DE and ARMAND DE NIEUWENHOVE, "Un Diplomate en bleu marin" R. Julliard, Paris, 1961.

BECK, STUART "The Ship — How She Works" Adlard Coles Ltd., Shouthampton 1955.

BEESLEY, LAWRENCE, "The Loss of the S.S. Titanic", Houghton Miffin Co., Boston 1912.

BEMELMANS, LUDWIG, "I Love You, I Love You, I Love You" Viking Press, New York 1942.

BERNSTEAD C. R. "Atlantic Ferry" Methuen & Cdo., Ltd., London 1936.

BISSET, SIR JAMES "Commodore" Criterion Books, New York 1961.

BISSET, SIR JAMES "Ship Ahoy!!" Charles Birchall Ltd., Liverpool, 1924.

BONSOR, M.P. "North Atlantic Seaway," Prescot, Lancashire, 1955

BOWEN, FRANK "A Century of Atlantic Travel 1830-1930" Little, Brown and Company, Boston, 1930.

BRADY, EDWARD MICHAEL, "Marine Salvage Operations" Cornell Maritime Press, New York, 1960.

BRAYNARD, FRANK O. "By Their Works Ye Shall Know Them", Gibbs & Cox, New York, 1968.

BRAYNARD, FRANK O. "Lives of the Liners" Cornell Maritime Press, New York, 1947.

BRAYNARD, FRANK O. "S.S. Savannah", University of Georgia Press,
    Athens, 1963.

BRINNIN, JOHN MALCOLM, "The Sway of the Grand Saloon" Delacorte Press,
    New York, 1971.

BROOK, RUPERT, "Letters from America", Charles Scribner's Sons,
    New York, 1916.

CAIRES, B. NICHOLAS T., "Passenger Liners of the World Since 1893" Bonanza
    Books, New York.

CANGARDEL, HENRI, "De J.-B Colbert Au Paquebot Normandie" Nouvelles
    Editions Latines, Paris 1957.

CECIL, LAMAR, "Albert Ballin" Princeton University Press, Princeton, 1967.

CHADWICK, F.E. et al. "Ocean Steamships" Charles Scribner's Sons,
    New York, 1891.

COEN, MARTIN J. "Ship Welding Handbook" Cornell Maritime Press,
    New York, 1943.

COOPER, DUFF, "Old Men Forget" Rupert Hart-Davis, London, 1953.

CORNWELL, E.L., "Illustrated History of Ships" Crescent Books, New York.

CORSI, EDWARD, "In the Shadow of Liberty", Mcmillan, New York, 1935.

CORSON, F. REID, "The Atlantic Ferry in the Twentieth Century" S. Low,
    Marston & Co. Ltd., London, 1930.

CRONICAN, FRANK and EDWARD A. MUELLER, "The Stateliest Ship", The
    Steamship Historical Society of America, New York, n.d.

DAVIS, CHARLES, G., "Ships of the Past", Bonanza Books, New York.

DIGGLE, E.G., "The Romance of a Modern Liner" S. Low, Marston & Co. Ltd,
    London, 1930.

DUGAN, JAMES, "The Great Iron Ship" Harper & Brothers, New York, 1953.

DUNN, LAURENCE, "North Atlantic Liners 1899-1913" H. Evelyn,
    London, 1961.

DUNN, LAURENCE "Passenger Liners" Adlard Coles, Southampton, 1961.

EISELE, PETER T. "Steamboat Bill" Journal of the Steamship Historical Society
    of America, New York.

ELLSBERG, EDWARD, "The Far Shore" Dodd, Mead, New York, 1960.

FILBY, P. WILLIAM, "Passenger and Immigration Lists Bibligoraphy 1538-1900",
    Gale Research Company, Michigan.

FLEMING, THE REVEREND JOHN, "The Last Voyage of His Majesty's Hospital
    Ship Britannic" n.d.

FLETCHER, R.A., "Travelling Palaces" Sir Isaac Pitman and Sons, Ltd.,
    London, 1913.

FLEXNER, J.T., "Steamboats Come True" Viking Press, New York, 1944.

FORWOOD, WILLIAM B., "Reminiscences of a Liverpool Shipowner" H. Young
    & Sons, Ltd., Liverpool, 1920.

GENEALOGICAL PUBLISHING COMPANY, INC. "Morton Allan Directory of
    European Passenger Ship Arrivals 1890-1930", 1980.

GENEALOGICAL PUBLISHING COMPANY, INC., "Passenger Arrivals of the
    Port of Baltimore 1820-1834", 1982.

GERMANS FROM RUSSIA HERITAGE SOCIETY, "Heritage Review" North
    Dakota, 1982.

GIBBS, C.R. VERNON, "Passenger Liners of the Western Ocean" Staples Press Ltd., London, 1952.

GOLDING, HARRY, ed. "The Wonder Book of Ships" Ward Locke & Company, London 14th ed.

GRACIE, ARCHIBALD, "The Truth about the Titanic" M. Kennerley, New York, 1913.

GRAHAM, JOHN MAXTONE "The Only Way to Cross" Collier Books.

GRATTIDGE, HARVEY, "Captain of the Queens" E.P. Dutton & Co., New York, 1956.

GREENHILL, BASIL and ANN GIFFORD, "Victorian and Edwardian Merchant Steamships" Naval Release, Annapolis.

HARTLEY, HERBERT, "Home is the Sailor" as told to Clint Bonner, Vulcan Press, Birmingham, 1955.

HAYES, SIR BERTRAM "Hull Down" E.P. Dutton & Co., New York, 1925.

HOCKING, CHARLES, "Dictionary of Disasters at Sea During the Age of Steam 1824-1962" Lloyd's Register of Shipping, London.

HOEHLING, ADOLPH and MARY, "The Last Voyage of the Lusitania" Henry Hold and Company, New York, 1956.

HOFF, RHODA, "America's Immigrants" Henry Z. Walch, New York, 1967.

HOMES, CAMPBELL, "Practical Shipbuilding" Longman Green & Co., London, 1904.

HULDERMANN, BERNHARD, "Albert Ballin" translated by W.J. Eggers, Cassell & Co., London, 1922.

HURD, SIR ARCHIBALD, "The Merchant Navy" volumes I, II & III, John Murray, London, 1921-1929.

ISHERWOOD, J.H., "Steamers of the Past" Sea Breezes, Liverpool, 1966.

JACKSON, GEORGE GIBBARD, "Steamships: Their History and Their Deeds" The Boy's Own Paper Office, London. n.d.

JACKSON, GEORGE GIBBARD, "The Story of the Liner" The Sheldon Press, London, 1931.

JORDON, HUMPHREY, "Mauretania" Hodder & Stoughton, London, 1936.

KELLEY, J.D. JERROLD, "The Ship's Company" Harper & Brothers Publishers, New York, 1897.

KEMP, PETER, "Encyclopedia of Ships and Seafaring" Crown Publishers, Inc., New York.

LADAGE, JOHN H., "Modern Ships" Cornell Maritime Press, New York, 1953.

LANCOUR, HAROLD and WOLFE, RICHARD J. "A Bibliography of Ship Passenger Lists 1538-1825" New York Public Library.

LANIER, EDMOND, "Compagnie Generale Transatlantique", Plon, Paris, 1962.

LAURIET, CHARLES E., "The Lusitania's Last Voyage" Houghton Mifflin Company, Boston and New York, 1915.

LAWRENCE, JACK, "When the Ships Came In" Farrar & Rinehart Inc., New York, 1940.

LEDOUX, KATHERINE R., "Ocean Notes for Ladies" G.P. Putnam's Sons, New York, 1877.

LEE, CHARLES E., "The Blue Riband" S. Low, Marston & Co., Ltd, London, 1930.

LIGHTOLLER, CHARLES E., "Titanic and Other Ships" I. Nicholson and Watson, Ltd., London, 1935.

LOBLEY, DOUGLAS, ed., "The Cunarders 1840-1969" Peter Barker Publishing Ltd., London, 1969.

LORD, WALTER, "A Night to Remember" Holt, Rinehart and Winston, New York, 1955.

MACDOUGAL, MICHAEL, "Gamblers Don't Gamble" as told to J.C. Furnas, The Greystone Press, New York, 1939.

MAGINNIS, ARTHUR J. "The Atlantic Ferry" Whittaker & Co., 1892.

MARCUS, GEOFFREY, "The Maiden Voyage" George Allen and Unwin Ltd. Londin, 1969.

MASTERS, DAVID, "Epics of Salvage" Cassell & Co., Ltd. London, 1953.

MCNEIL, SAMUEL, "In Great Waters" Faber & Faber, Ltd., London, 1932.

MEIER, FRANK, "Fathoms Below" E.P. Dutton & Co., New York, 1943.

MILLER, BYRON S., "Sail, Steam & Spendour" The New York Times Book Company.

MILLER, JOHN F., "American Ships of the Colonial & Revolutionary Period" W.W. Norton Co. Inc., New York.

MILLER, WILLIAM H. Jr., "The Great Luxury Liners 1927-1954" Dover Publications, Inc., New York, 1981.

MORRIS, JAMES, "The Great Port" a Helen and Kurt Wolff Book, Harcourt, Brace & World, Inc. New York, 1969.

MOSCOW, ALVIN, "Collision Course" G.P. Putnam's Sons, New York, 1959.

NEVETT, CEDRIC RIDGELY, "American Steamships on the Atlantic" University of Delaware Press.

NEWELL, GORDON, "Ocean Liners of the 20th Century" Superior Publishing Co. Seattle, 1963.

NIEZYCHOUSKI, ALFRED VON, "The Cruise of the Kronprinz Wilhelm" Doubleday, Doran E. Company, Inc., Garden City, N.Y., 1929.

NOVOTNY, ANN, "Strangers at the Door" Chatham Press, Riverside, 1971.

OLDHAM, WILTON, J., "The Ismay Line" Charles Birchall and Sons Ltd. Liverpool, 1961.

OWEN, H., "Ship Economics" G. Phillip & Sons, London, 1911.

PADFIELD, PETER, "An Agony of Collisions" Hodder and Stoughton, London, 1966.

PADFIELD, PETER, "The Titanic and the Californian" Hodder and Stoughton, London, 1965.

POTTER, NEIL and JACK FROST, "The Elizabeth" George C. Harrap & Co. Ltd., London, 1965.

POTTER, NEIL and JACK FROST, "The Mary" George G. Harrap & Co. Ltd., London, 1961.

POTTER, NEIL and JACK FROST, "Queen Elizabeth 2" George G. Harrap & Co. Ltd., London, 1969.

RIMINGTON, CRITCHELL, "The Bon Voyage Book" John Day Company, New York, 1931.

ROSSELL, HENRY E. and LAWRENCE B. CHAPMAN, eds. "Principles of Naval Architecture" The Society of Naval Architects and Marine Engineers, New York, 1941.

SASSOON, SIEGRIELD, "Siegfried's Journey" Viking Press, New York, 1946.

SIMPSON, GEORGE, "The Naval Constructor", D. Van Nostrand Co. New York, 1914.

SMITH, EUGENE W., "Passengers Ships of the World, Past and Present", 2nd ed. George H. Dean Company, Boston.

SPEDDING, CHARLES T. "Reminiscences of Transatlantic Travelers", J.B. Lipincott Co. Philadelphia, 1926.

SPRATT. H.P. "Outline History of Transatlantic Steam Navigation" The Science Museum, London, 1950.

SPRATT, H.P., "The Merchant Steamers and Motor Ships" The Science Museum, London, 1950.

SPURGEON, SIR ARTHUR, "The Burning of the Volturno" Cassell & Co., Ltd., London, 1913.

STANFORD, DON, "Ile de France" Appleton-Century-Crofts, Inc. New York, 1960.

STEVENS, LEONARD A., "The Elizabeth: Passage of a Queen" Alfred A. Knopf, New York, 1968.

STEVENSON, ROBERT LOUIS, "The Amateur Emigrant" Charles Scribner's Sons, New York, 1911.

STREET, JULIAN, "Ship-Bored" Dodd Mead & Co., New York, 1924.

TALBOT, FREDERICK A., "Steamship Conquest of the World" J.B. Lippincott Co. Philadelphia, 1926.

TAYLOR, DAVID B. "Steam Conquers the Atlantic" Appleton-Century Company, New York, and London, 1939.

THAYER, JOHN B., "The Sinking of the S.S. Titanic April 14th-15th 1912" Philadelphia, 1912.

THOMPSON, FRANK E., "Diving, Cutting and Welding in Underwater Salvage Operations" Cornell Maritime Press, New York, 1944.

THOREUX, PIERRE, "J'ai Commande Normandie" Presses de la Cite Paris, 1957.

TURC. C. "Le navire pour passengers" E. Bernard & Cie, Paris, 1903.

TUTE, WARREN, "Atlantic Conquest" Little, Brown and Company, Boston, 1962.

VILLIERS, ALAN, "The Western Ocean" Museum Press, London, 1957.

WHEELER, GEORGE JAMES, "Ship Salvage" E.W. Sweetman, New York, 1958.

WHITE, E.B., "Here is New York" Haper & Brothers, New York, 1949.

WILSON, R.M., "The Big Ships" Cassell & Co., Ltd., London, 1956.

WILSON, V.S. FELLOWS, "The Largest Ships in the World" Crosby Lockwood & Son, London, 1926.

WITTHOFT, HANS JURGEN, "Norddeutscher Lloyd" Koehlers Verlagsgesellichoft Herford.

WOON, BASIL, "The Frantic Atlantic" Alfred Knopf, New York, 1927.

YOUNG, FILSON, "Titanic" G. Richards, London, 1912.
"Merchant Steam Vessels of the United States 1790-1868"

INDEX